Wild Food

for Phoebe Foy Phillips

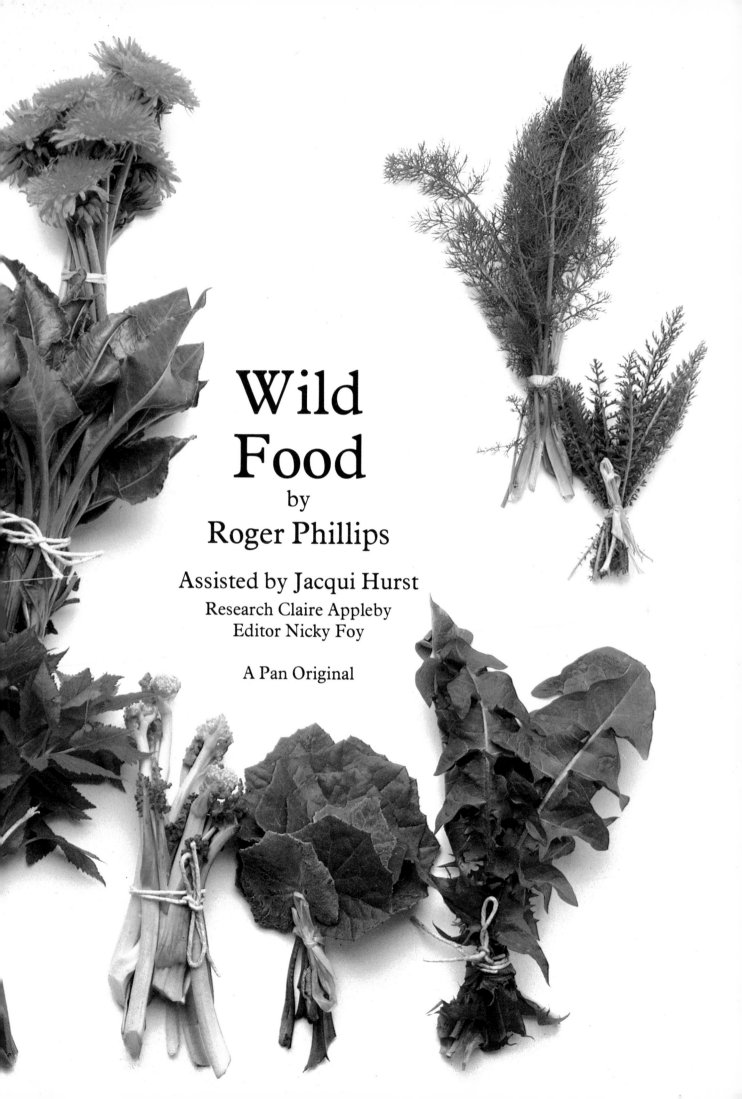

Wild
Food

by
Roger Phillips

Assisted by Jacqui Hurst

Research Claire Appleby
Editor Nicky Foy

A Pan Original

Acknowledgements

I would like to thank the following people who gave me help
with the recipes that appear in this book:
Mrs Aggies, Susan and Dede Alnut, Gunvor Avery, Marie
Lou Avery, Beverley Behrens, Steven Bull, Kyle Cathie,
Yvonne and Stan Cocking, Ray Cowell, Mary, Emma and
Danny Dalton, Frank Duke and Honor, Nina
Edwards, Maureen Elworthy, Ted Green,
Jane Grigson, Hazel Hurst, Geoffrey Kibby,
Paul Levy, Meinhard Moser, Mary Norwak,
Kate Penoyre, Elsie Phillips, Stephan Pierce,
Simon Plant, Alice and Wilfred Preston,
Mervyn Rayner, Martyn Rix, Ted Rix,
Sharon Shute, Janie Southering, Katie
Stewart, Geoff and Jenny Stone,
Ben Turner, Simon and Caroline Ward,
Stan and Pammy Williams.

I am most grateful to the following for the use of the
photographs that have been included: Jacqui Hurst – Marsh
Samphire 95, Sea Pen 95, Bullace 132, Cortinarious
purpurascens 140, Rosa rugosa 143, Blue Legs 153. Martyn
Rix – Cowberry 101.

Thanks are due to Sue Rose for her work on the layout.

Thanks are also due to a great many magazines, authors,
publishers and institutions. I hope I have given them all the
appropriate credit in the text.

Contents

Introduction

In producing this book, I have tried to do two things which I felt had not been covered before in one volume.

Firstly, I wanted to make sure that the book could be used as a basic reference for all the most well-known recipes traditionally associated with wild food (such as blackberry jam, dandelion coffee, angelica, lime tea, elderflower wine, etc.) and so I have included all the standard recipes. But secondly, I wanted to go further than this. By exploring and developing some of the other fascinating sources of wild food, such as seaweeds and mushrooms, I could show that there are several areas that have been left largely unexploited and yet they provide a great many of the most delicious and nutritious recipes for the adventurous hunter's table.

Two principles have guided my choices throughout. I have only included those plants which can be found in sufficiently large quantities to make eating them worthwhile and, much more importantly, to ensure that taking a collection of them will not endanger the survival of any population of the species. Furthermore, I have tried to select a definitive recipe for each plant rather than list all possible recipes. The sense of this will be seen if you think of mushrooms. There are just under fifty species dealt with in the book and yet most of the recipes could be interchanged. The actual recipe selected for each species is the one that, after numerous testing-and-tasting sessions, I think best suits the flavour and texture of that particular mushroom.

The recipes have been gleaned from a variety of sources. Historical research into old herbals and cookery books revealed an enormous number of ideas about how to cook wild plants, many far too elaborate and impracticable for modern cooks, but nevertheless fascinating reading. I am also indebted to numerous contemporary authors and magazines for recipes I have either quoted verbatim or adapted slightly to suit my ingredients; and last, but by no means least, I have regularly invaded the kitchens of friends and acquaintances to steal their cherished secrets.

As a result of this research, I collected a wide range of recipes – far more than could possibly be used. So, in order to find out which ones I personally liked the best, I made every single recipe and only included in the book those that seemed really worthwhile, even though it meant rejecting about two-thirds of the material. The exception to this rule has been the inclusion of a few medieval recipes, which have been inserted for interest only.

How to use this book

Following the format I used in my book *Wild Flowers of Britain and Europe,* the arrangement of the plants in this book is chronological. This means that if you are going wild food hunting in the spring, you can look in the early part of the book at ideas of plants to search for and you will find recipes appropriate to those plants. Conversely, if you collect some interesting berries or mushrooms in the autumn you can look in the book's later sections for ideas of what to do with them. However, should you want to look up a particular recipe or plant, the index, which lists both common and botanical names, will guide you to the entries.

Seaweeds

The seaweeds must be, without doubt, the most wasted of our natural resources. In the past a few species have been eaten but generally speaking the habit has died out, although laver in Wales and carragheen in Ireland are still consumed in some quantity. Perhaps the reason why the edible seaweeds have disappeared from our tables is because the standard ways of cooking them emerged out of necessity and poverty, rather than from choice and taste.

I have spent a great deal of time comparing our species of seaweed to those eaten in Japan and discovered that we have many species that are almost identical and ours are just as succulent and delicious to eat. So, apart from the traditional recipes, the majority of those included here have been adapted from Japanese recipes or from West Coast American recipes, most of which have been brought over from Japan anyway.

A small selection of dried mushrooms from the jars in my kitchen.

Kitchen scissors and garden gloves take the sting out of nettle collecting.

Seaweeds are among the most nutritious plants that can be found as they contain high proportions of vitamins, proteins and minerals. Vitamins A, B_1, B_{12}, C and D are contained in large quantities in many seaweeds. Sea lettuce, for instance, has more of the 'growth vitamin', vitamin A, than butter and many of the green seaweeds contain a higher concentration of vitamin B_{12} than can be found in liver. Seaweeds contain about 2.5 per cent of protein by weight, so that laver, for instance, contains a higher proportion of protein than do soya beans. As well as this, all species of seaweed are rich in minerals and trace elements because sea water has almost exactly the same proportion of minerals as human blood.

Mushroom collecting

This book does not set out to be a field guide to the identification of edible mushrooms. There are in the region of 2000 mushrooms that may be found in Europe, including poisonous and edible species. Before actually considering eating wild mushrooms you must be sure of your identification; for this you will need a specialist book and/or the help of an expert. However, if you persevere and conquer the problems you will find cooking and eating wild mushrooms opens up many new, exciting and rewarding culinary areas to explore.

In choosing mushroom recipes I have tried to sort out one appropriate to each of the species covered but these recipes are in no way meant to be exclusive to one species. Once you have become adept at finding and naming mushrooms, you often discover that at the end of an afternoon's searching, you have a mixed bag of perhaps eight or ten edible species. Most dishes are enhanced by a *mélange* of fungi so just pick any of the recipes in the book and try it with the mushrooms you've collected.

Botanical information

This book does not set out to be a flora for the identification of wild plants and fungi; that job must, of necessity, be left to specialist works. I have confined myself, therefore, to information on times of growth, flowering and fruiting, habitat and distribution.

The Latin name and its authority have been included for every entry as I found that there were many cases where clarification was necessary. What, for example, is the difference between oregano and marjoram, blueberries and bilberries, the two kinds of fennel? I hope that this approach will prove helpful and clear up some of the problems in relation to these and other difficult groups of species.

Protection of wild plants

It is my firm belief that increased knowledge and interest in the flora of our countryside will lead to greater personal thought about how wild plants may be best protected and encouraged. This statement might seem to be at odds with a book about the collection and consumption of wild plants, fruits and roots, but man cannot live without eating and, as I have already pointed out, I have only included recipes for plants which are in no danger of extinction. It is a fact that the greatest threat to the continuing destruction of our wild flora is caused by loss of habitat, due to building, road-making, draining and farming. Careful collection of wild plants is not of itself an ecological menace.

I would like to emphasize again to the prospective wild food hunter that only plants which are growing in profusion should be harvested and then only in such quantities that the viability of each colony will not be endangered.

Please remember that all plants are now protected under the law. Firstly, it is illegal to uproot any plant without the permission of the landowner and furthermore there is a list of 62 plants that may not be picked under any circumstances. (None of them is in this book.) For a list of these plants and further information on the conservation of wild plants, write to: The Nature Conservancy Council, 19 Belgrave Square, London SW1.

Herbs, flowers, seaweeds and fungi are easy to preserve by drying.

Bottling home-made wine may be time-consuming but sampling the 'left overs' makes it most enjoyable.

Drying

Drying is a most useful method of preserving, especially for herbs, seaweeds and mushrooms. I have found the most practical and effective method is to rig up a wire rack about 8 cm (3 in) above a radiator; this allows a good current of hot air to flow around the material and enables things to dry very quickly. Mushrooms which contain more than 90 per cent moisture should be cut into slices to speed up the drying process. Keep the dried mushrooms in a jar with a good seal in a warm, dry place. If, however, you live in a damp house, this will be a waste of time as the material will quickly regain moisture and deteriorate.

Wine making

There are two approaches that can be taken to making wines from wild fruits and flowers. The first aims to preserve the taste and flavour of the specific flower or fruit that has been collected, while the second is to produce a wine which is as near as possible to a commercial wine made from grapes. I prefer the first approach and so, in every instance, I have balanced the ingredients to bring out the essential taste of the fruit or flowers that are the main constituent. The result, I hope, is a series of wines that have really authentic country flavours. All the recipes in this book have been designed to give a dry wine with general purpose yeast.

Yeast: This is generally available from chemists, specialist shops and large stores. I have used a general purpose yeast for both wine and beer. It can be 'started' very rapidly by putting the contents of the packet into a mug, with a little sugar and warm water, and then leaving in a warm place for about an hour. There are also special wine yeasts available; such yeasts will possibly be able to work out a larger proportion of sugars and thus make a higher alcohol content. If you decide to give these yeasts a try, add a little more sugar to my recipes. Wine yeasts are normally much more difficult to start.

Cloudy wine: If your wine will not clear, despite being given plenty of time after the fermentation has ceased, the most likely cause is either a starch haze or a pectin haze, both of which can be detected with a simple test. Starch dyes dark brown in iodine, so if you put a few drops of the cloudy wine in a glass and then add a drop of iodine, there will be a distinct darkening if starch is present. Pectin can easily be discerned by adding a few drops of the wine to a very small quantity of methylated spirits which should then be shaken and left for a few minutes. If pectin is present it will group itself together to form whitish clots. Both types of haze may easily be dealt with: if you detect a starch haze, buy an amylase enzyme and if you have a pectin haze, buy 'pectinol'. Use as instructed.

Sterilization: This is essential because wine-making vessels that have not been properly sterilized are the most common cause of failure in wine making. A strong solution of campden tablets can be used for this purpose, or proprietary brands of cleaning and sterilizing powder are available from the specialist wine-making shops. Sterilize corks by boiling them for 15 minutes.

The photographs

All the photographs, except those on the title pages, have been taken in natural light using a Nikon FM camera with a 50 mm lens on a tripod. The film used was Kodak Ektachrome 64 ASA which was pushed one stop in development. This enabled me to stop the lens down to f16 and yet not have to use too slow a shutter speed, thus reducing wind movement.

I have endeavoured, wherever possible, to take the recipe photographs in conjunction with the plants from which the dishes were made and in the natural habitat of the plants. Obviously, this required a lot of travelling and hard work, but it gave me the opportunity of doing food photographs against a great variety of lovely, natural backgrounds, which made working on this book continuously exciting, interesting and stimulating.

Bittercress has a sharp, hot flavour like watercress. It is excellent in sandwiches as an adjunct to cheese. Photographed March 1.

Hairy Bittercress *Cardamine hirsuta* L. The first worthwhile edible plant to be found at the beginning of the year, it is an annual herb common throughout the British Isles. It occurs on bare ground (particularly on the bare soil of flower beds), in gardens and on ploughed arable fields and it can also be found on rocks, screes, walls etc. It flowers from March to September but the leaves can be eaten from October until May.

Common wintercress or **Yellow Rocket** *Barbarea vulgaris* R.Br. Common wintercress occurs throughout Great Britain, being common in the south but less frequent further north. It may be biennial or perennial and it grows in hedges, stream banks, waysides and other damp places. It flowers from May to August.

Common wintercress was, in the past, commonly cultivated in English gardens as an early salad. In Sweden the leaves were boiled as kale, while in New Zealand the natives used the plant as a food under the name *toi*. In the 17th century, John Pechey said of the plant, ''Tis acrid and hote, and much of the same Virtue with Cresses. 'Tis mix'd with Sallets, especially in the Winter-time, when Cresses are scarce; wherefore 'tis called Winter-Cress.'

I find it makes a super vegetable lightly boiled. In salads it is a nice, rather hot-flavoured addition, similar to watercress. To increase the plant's productivity remove the flowering stems as they appear and pick the outer leaves as the plant re-grows.

Chickweed *Stellaria media* (L.) Vill. An annual or overwintering herb abundant throughout the British Isles, which occurs on cultivated ground and waste places. Chickweed can be found all the year round but is not worth using in high summer when it becomes straggly and dusty. It comes into its own with the onset of autumn and often remains in good condition until destroyed by heavy frosts. A fine new growth starts at the very beginning of spring.

The whole plant can be eaten. Gather using scissors rather than pulling it up, pick clean and lay neatly in a basket as this saves much preparation time later on.

Chickweed Salad

SERVES TWO
1 large bunch chickweed
3 tablespoons French dressing
3 teaspoons chopped, wild chervil
2 crisp apples, chopped into cubes

Wash the chickweed and mix with the apples. Add the chervil to the French dressing and blend. Pour the dressing over the salad and toss lightly.

Chickweed Soup

SERVES SIX
1½ litres (2½ pints) chicken stock
6 spring onions, white and green parts, thinly sliced
1 large potato, peeled and diced
2 bunches chickweed, trimmed, washed and with any tough stems removed (reserve a few sprigs for a garnish)
Salt
Freshly ground pepper
3 dl (½ pint) cream

Put the stock into a large, heavy saucepan and bring to boiling point. Lower the heat. Add the onions, potato and chickweed and simmer, covered, for 10 to 15 minutes. Do not overcook or the soup will lose its flavour. Season with salt and pepper then purée in a blender. Return to the saucepan and add the cream. Heat through but do not boil. Garnish with a few sprigs of the chickweed and serve hot.

This is a delicious soup and as the chickweed can be so readily found in abundance it is well worth trying. I like it with the addition of a few sorrel leaves if they are about.

Winter Herb Salad

SERVES TWO-FOUR
1 large bunch mixed winter salad herbs: wintercress, bittercress and chickweed
2 oranges
4 tablespoons olive oil
1 tablespoon wine vinegar
1 tablespoon lemon juice
Salt
Freshly ground pepper
1 finely chopped shallot

Wash the salad herbs and peel the oranges, discarding all the skin and pith, then cut into segments. Chill. Put the olive oil, vinegar, lemon juice, seasoning and shallot into a screw-topped jar. Shake until well blended. Just before serving, arrange the salad herbs and orange segments in a salad bowl. Pour the dressing over and mix well.

Common wintercress, a succulent early spring vegetable. Photographed March 29.

Chickweed as a salad has a flavour similar to lettuce. Cooked in a soup it is excellent. Photographed March 10.

Birch sap is much quicker and easier to collect than you would imagine; you get about 2½ litres (4 pints) overnight. To make sure you don't harm the tree, hammer in a wooden peg when you have finished. Photographed March 15.

Silver Birch *Betula alba* L. The name 'birch' is a very ancient one, probably derived from the Sanskrit *bhurga* meaning 'a tree whose bark is used for writing upon'. The birch was a protective tree, used to avert the evil eye. In particular, on Midsummer Eve it was thought lucky to hang birch boughs over the doors of houses and, in Scotland, over signposts in the town. At one time a birch broomstick or besom wedding was thought perfectly legal. The couple jumped, one at a time, over a birch broom held against the doorway of their house and they were then regarded as married. An old English proverb, referring to the winter appearance of the tree, says, 'He is as bare as the birch at Yule even'.

The birch has been put to many uses in the country. John Pechey, writing in the 17th century, describes some of these: 'The slender twigs of it were formerly used for the Magistrates Verge; Now they serve to discipline Boys, and to tame wild horses, and to make Brooms . . . Fishermen in Northumberland fish a-nights by the Light of this Bark: They put it into a cleft stick, which serves for a Candle-stick; and so they see how to use their Three-teeth'd Spear for killing Fish.' The twigs have been employed for thatching and making wattles and the sap has been used to make various beverages such as beer, wine, spirit and vinegar.

Birch Sap Wine

4½ litres (8 pints) sap
200 g (½ lb) chopped raisins
1 kg (2¼ lb) white sugar
Juice of 2 lemons
General purpose yeast

Boil the sap as soon after collecting as possible as it can very easily go off. Add the sugar to the boiling liquid and simmer for 10 minutes. Place the chopped raisins in a polythene bucket, pour the boiling liquid onto them and add the lemon juice. Start the yeast in a glass. Leave until the mixture cools to blood heat, then add the started yeast. Leave to ferment in the covered bucket for three days and then strain off into a 4.5 litre (1 gallon) jar and seal with an air lock. Leave in a warm room or cupboard until fermentation ceases. At this stage rack off the wine into a clean jar and leave it until the sediment has settled or, as I normally do, filter the wine to remove the sediment. Bottle in clean, sterilized bottles, cork and store in a cool place. This wine may be drunk after a month or so but it is even better after six months. If at the bottling stage the wine is too dry, I normally sweeten it with a very little sugar syrup before bottling, but be careful not to oversweeten it.

Collecting Sap

Take sap from mature trees during the first two weeks of March. Bore a hole, the width of your tube, slanting upwards about 18 inches from the ground, and insert a piece of plastic tubing to lead down into a collecting bottle through a bung made of tissue paper. Be sure to cork up the hole in the tree firmly after you have collected your sap so that the tree does not bleed to death.

Collection is much easier than it sounds. I collected over 2 litres in 24 hours. However, it is important to ensure a tight fit between the piping and the hole so that the sap all runs down into the jar and does not leak.

Sycamore *Acer pseudoplatanus* L. The sycamore is a deciduous tree, common throughout the British Isles, occurring in woods, hedges and plantations. It prefers deep, moist, well-drained, rich soils but will grow on all but very poor soils. It flowers from April to June.

The sycamore is believed to have been imported into Britain from France in the Middle Ages. It appears infrequently in folklore and tradition but there is one tale told of it by K. M. Briggs in his *Folklore of the Cotswolds*, 1974, as follows:
'There is a solitary sycamore by the roadside a mile or two from Dover known as the Lone Tree, and singular tradition attaches to it. A soldier of the garrison at Dover is said to have slain a comrade with a staff, and as the two men were alone he struck it into the ground, exclaiming that this would never be discovered until that dry staff took root. He served abroad for many years unsuspected,

but when once again stationed at Dover he visited the spot, driven by a morbid curiosity, and found that his staff had taken root and was a flourishing tree. Stricken with horror, he avowed his crime, and suffered for it on the gallows. The tree used to be visible from the ramparts at Dover, and it is stated that the story was traditional in the garrison.'

Sycamore Sap Wine

This is made in just the same way as the Birch Sap Wine though the sycamore gives a sweeter sap. I imagine an American Sugar Maple would make a superb sap wine as no doubt the sugar levels would be even higher. The sap is not as easy to collect as that from birch trees since the flow is not nearly as strong.

Pennywort is common on old walls in the west country. Only pick the leaves when you find it in profusion. Photographed April 27.

Pennywort or **Navelwort** *Umbilicus rupestris* (Salisb.) Dandy. A common, native plant of the west of England, Wales and southern Ireland, rare elsewhere, found growing in rocky crevices and especially on old walls.

The fleshy leaves are useful for salads or as an addition to sandwiches but please only pick them when you find them in profusion.

Ivy-leaved toadflax can be found almost all year round. Photographed March 28.

Ivy-leaved Toadflax *Cymbalaria muralis* Gaertn., Mey & Scherb. A common native plant of England, Wales and Ireland but rare in north Scotland, it is found on walls and flowers from May to September. The fleshy little leaves can be eaten in salads.

Preparing morels à la crème, with a string of dried morels, in the ivy under ash trees where they were found.

Morels *Morchella.* One of the most prized and sought-after of the whole fungus flora, they normally occur from March to May in loose sandy soil, overlying chalk. They must be very carefully prepared before cooking to make sure that no wood lice, earwigs or other tiny creatures are lurking in the cavities. Cut each morel in half, top to bottom, and remove the base of the stem. Wash under a running tap and then drop each piece into boiling water for a few seconds to blanch them.

To Dry Morels

Cut the morels in half and wash them carefully, removing the base of the stem. Dry them with a towel, thread on to strings and hang them up to dry in a warm kitchen or over a radiator. When they are dry and crisp, after a day or two, take down and keep in a sealed jar in a warm, dry place. To reconstitute, just soak them in water for half an hour. They retain their flavour very well and can be used in place of fresh ones without any loss of quality.

Morels à la Crème

Jane Grigson, in her excellent book *Mushroom Feast*, has this recipe for morels that she believes to be the dish mentioned in the *Alice B. Toklas Cook Book*. I made it in individual-sized flan cases and it was superb, but made in a large flan case it is equally good, if not better.

SERVES SIX-EIGHT
Pastry:
50 g (2 oz) butter
100 g (4 oz) flour
1 teaspoon salt
1 egg
2 tablespoons double cream

Sauce Mornay:
30 g (1 generous oz) butter
1 medium onion, sliced
1 medium carrot, sliced
1 stalk celery, sliced
Salt, pepper
1 heaped tablespoon flour
6 dl (1 pint) hot milk
3 tablespoons double cream

Mushrooms:
500 g (1 lb) morels
25 g (1 oz) butter
Juice of ½ lemon
1 tablespoon sherry
Salt, pepper, paprika
½ clove garlic, crushed

To make the pastry, rub the butter into the flour, then add the salt and egg. Gently knead into a ball, sprinkle with flour and roll out. Spread half the cream over it, knead and roll out again. Add the remaining cream, knead and roll out, then roll into a ball. Leave in the refrigerator for an hour, then use pastry to line a flan tin with a removable base and bake blind for about 10 minutes in a 200°C (400°F, Mark 6) oven.

Meanwhile make the sauce Mornay. Melt butter and fry the vegetables in it until lightly browned; add seasoning and flour. Cook gently for 5 minutes, then stir in the hot milk. Simmer for half an hour until the sauce is reduced to a rather thicker consistency than normal for a pouring sauce. Strain into a clean bowl, then add cream.

To prepare the mushrooms, cook them in the butter, lemon juice, sherry, salt, pepper, paprika and garlic for 8 minutes, covered. Remove mushrooms with a perforated spoon and add to the sauce Mornay. Pour into the baked flan case and place in a 230°C (450°F, Mark 8) oven for 12 minutes. Keep an eye on it to make sure it does not burn.

This is a superb dish that will reward all the effort of preparation.

Photographed April 20.

15

*Common morel **Morchella vulgaris** (Pers.) Boud. This is our most common morel. It is to be found on sandy soil, usually overlying chalk, in gardens or on wasteland or wood edges, especially in East Anglia. Photographed April 15.*

Morchella esculenta Pers. ex. St Amans. This is the favourite of the edible morels usually found in association with ash but also sometimes with apple or elm. Photographed April 8.

Morels on Fried Bread

SERVES FOUR AS A FIRST COURSE
250 g (½ lb) morels
50 g (2 oz) butter
Parsley and thyme
1 egg yolk
3 tablespoons double cream
Bread

Wash and clean the caps in running water, remove the stem bases, dry thoroughly and split longitudinally. Stew them for about 30 minutes in butter with a little stock, chopped parsley and thyme, pepper and salt. Thicken with the whipped egg yolk mixed with the cream. Serve on fried bread.

This really is a delicious dish, much more exciting than it sounds.

'Fricassy of Morelles'

Carter in his *Herbal* publication of 1730 has the following recipe: 'If you have them Green, you must cleanse them from the Sand by washing them, and brown a Piece of Butter Gold Colour, and toss them up, and their own Liquor will stove them; season them only with Pepper, Salt and Nutmeg, and an Onion, and a little minc'd Parsley; when stov'd tender, toss them up as a Fricassy, with the Yolk of an Egg and a little White Wine, and a little Cream and thick Butter, and so serve them; and you may garnish with Lemon: If you use the dry ones, you must soak them in warm Water, and ragoust them off Brown with Gravy thicken'd, and season'd as

before; or you may toss them up likewise as a Fricassy, with the same Ingredients, White; and the large ones you may force with a light Forc'd meat of a Sweet-bread lightly season'd and broil'd in a butter'd Paper, roll'd up and serv'd in the Papers, and they will eat very well thus; but they must be first set, and then forc'd.'

Mousse Chaude aux Morilles

SERVES FOUR
4 large morels, washed very thoroughly
100 g (4 oz) white mushrooms
2 large chicken breasts, boned
1½ dl (¼ pint) double cream
3 dl (½ pint) velouté sauce (béchamel + chicken stock)
1 tablespoon Madeira
35 g (1½ oz) butter
Salt and black pepper

Liberally butter the inside of four teacups. Cut one morel into quarters lengthways and each quarter into five pieces. Cook very lightly in 12 g (½ oz) of the butter. Place pieces inside the teacups equi-distant from each other. If you have no morel large enough, cut up a smaller one similarly and simply place it, star-fashion, in the bottom of the teacup.

Filling: Chop the remaining morels (with their stalks) and the other mushrooms very finely and cook gently in the rest of the butter until the moisture has evaporated. Season and mix half with the velouté sauce and half the Madeira. Cool.

Mousse chaude aux morilles. An elaborate but quite exquisite dish. Photographed April 20.

Mousse: Finely chop the chicken breasts, trimmed of all sinew, or put in food processor for twenty seconds. Pass this, with the other half of the mushroom mixture, through a sieve into a small bowl. Place over some ice cubes and water in a large bowl and refrigerate for half an hour. Then, salt the mixture lightly and little by little beat in the chilled cream. Check for the right degree of saltiness. Divide the mousse into four and line each teacup with it to a thickness of 1.2 cm (½ in), making sure the morel pieces remain in place, leaving enough mousse to cover the top.

Fill the cavities with the chopped mushroom mixture and spread the remaining mousse over the top. Bake in a bain-marie in a medium oven 180°C (350°F, Mark 4) for half an hour, turn out and serve with the rest of the Madeira-flavoured sauce poured around.

This recipe came to me from Stephen Bull, the chef and proprietor of Lichfields Restaurant in Richmond. It is superb.

Nettle beer. It only takes one week from picking to drinking and makes a light, refreshing, ginger beer-type drink. Also shown in this picture – nettles as a vegetable. Photographed by the river Colne, March 6.

Stinging Nettle *Urtica dioica* L. A perennial herb, abundant and generally distributed throughout the British Isles, it occurs in hedgebanks, woods, grassy places, fens, and near buildings, especially where the ground is covered with litter or rubble. It flowers from May to October but should be picked by the beginning of June as in high summer the leaves become coarse in texture and bitter in taste, due to a chemical change.

The best time to collect them is when the young shoots are no more than a few centimetres high. Pick the whole of these shoots or, if gathering later in the year, just the tops and the young, pale green leaves. Wear gloves and cut the nettles with scissors, laying them tidily in a basket to facilitate sorting later on. During the summer suitable vegetation may be available where earlier growth has been cut back and a second crop of stems is growing. Before cooking, remove any tough stems and wash well.

A broth of water, nettles, salt, milk and oatmeal, called Brotchan Neanntog, was a favourite Irish dish from at least early Christian times until the cabbage became popular, less than 200 years ago. Many of the poorer people still relied on Brotchan Neanntog to a considerable extent in the earlier part of this century. In Scotland, nettles were grown under glass as 'early kale' while the wild variety was popular in broths, porridge and haggis.

Nettles contain iron, formic acid, ammonia, silicic acid and histamine. These chemicals aid the relief of rheumatism, sciatica and allied ailments. They increase the haemoglobin in the blood, improve the circulation, purify the system and have a generally toning effect on the whole body. Nettles also lower the blood pressure and the blood sugar level.

The stinging characteristics of the nettle gave rise to several proverbs, for example the 1753 'Nettle's Lesson':

> *Tender-handed stroke a nettle,*
> *And it stings you for your pains;*
> *Grasp it like a man of mettle,*
> *And it soft as silk remains.*

During the war I went to a village school run by a wonderful Bohemian woman called Miss Raymond. There were only about six children over the age of six – the rest of the school consisted of babies. Anyway, in common with the rest of the country, there was very little to eat at that time, so we six were sent out every morning to pick nettle tops which were boiled by the cook into a most unsavoury pulp. Then, when it was time for the babies' lunch, the long-suffering six had to attempt to push it down the babies' gullets – the babies, quite rightly, explosively rejected it, usually into the face of the feeder. I offer you nettles as a vegetable; believe it or not, I love them now!

Nettle Beer

100 nettle stalks (with leaves)
12 litres (2½ gallons) water
1½ kg (3 lb) sugar
50 g (2 oz) cream of tartar
15 g (½ oz) yeast

Boil nettles with 12 litres (2½ gallons) of water for 15 minutes. Strain, and add the sugar and the cream of tartar. Heat and stir until dissolved. Wait until tepid, then add the yeast and stir well. Cover with muslin and leave for 24 hours. Remove the scum and decant without disturbing the sediment. Bottle, cork and tie down.

I have made this many times and in practice it seems best to leave it to ferment in the bucket for 4 days, thus avoiding too much fizzing over when you open the bottles. Your first sip will dispel any doubts as to the excellence of this beer which makes a light, refreshing drink, ideal for serving on warm, early summer evenings. A sprig of mint and a cube of ice is worth adding when serving.

This recipe was given to me by Lindsay Shearer of Bucky who found it in the *Common Place Book* of her grandmother, Mary Buchan.

As a vegetable

Wash the fresh, young nettle sprigs and put into a saucepan without any additional water. Add a knob of butter and seasoning. Simmer gently for about ten minutes, turning all the time. The flavour is rather plain and so the addition of butter, nutmeg and black pepper is essential at the serving stage.

Conserve

John Hill, in his *Useful Family Herbal*, 1755, tells us that 'The flowers are the only part used, they are to be gather'd in May; and made up into Conserve. A Pound of them is to be beat up with two Pounds and a half of Sugar. They may also be dried.'

White Dead-Nettle *Lamium album* L. This perennial herb is common in England but very rare in Scotland north of the Caledonian canal. In Ireland it is found mainly in the east. It occurs in hedgebanks, roadsides and waste places and flowers from March to December.

This species was used as a vegetable in France until the last century and still occurs as an ingredient in some French dishes today. In Sweden it was formerly used as a pot herb and as herbal tea. Robinson says, 'It is an exhilarating herb, driving away melancholy, and it makes the heart merry.' It is also called Archangel because the flowers are supposed to open on the day dedicated to the Archangel Michael. As with the Stinging Nettle, it is best to use only fresh young shoots and leaves.

Red Dead-Nettle *Lamium purpureum* L. An annual herb, very common throughout the British Isles, which occurs on cultivated ground and waste places. It flowers from March until October. The young shoots should be collected carefully, using scissors. According to John Gerard, writing in the 16th century, the flowers could be 'baked with sugar, such as roses are'.

Red dead-nettle **Lamium purpureum** *is at its best in spring. It can be used in conjunction with other nettles. Photographed March 24.*

White dead-nettle **Lamium album** *can be found at all times of year but is at its best in early spring and late autumn. It can be used in place of stinging nettle. Photographed March 24.*

Nettle soup. My favourite soup in the book. Photographed in Shannagaray, Ireland, May 13. Nettles love to grow near ruins.

Cow parsley can be found from early spring but you should only use it if you are sure of its identification. Photographed March 30.

Long leaved scurvy grass is the most pleasant tasting of the group. Photographed March 13.

Cleavers. The leaves of cleavers are said to make a good vegetable but I find it bitter and unpleasant. Photographed March 10.

Common scurvy grass near the sea. Photographed July 18.

Nettle Soup

SERVES FOUR
1 large onion, 1 clove garlic
2 potatoes
2 gloved handfuls of nettle heads
Olive oil, salt and pepper
1 chicken stock cube
1.5 dl (¼ pint) single cream

Peel and chop the onion, garlic and potatoes and fry them for 3 or 4 minutes in a large saucepan in a little olive oil. Trim away the stems from the nettle tops using gloves and scissors, wash well and add them to the pan. Make up stock cube with 1 litre (1½ pints) of boiling water (or better still use home-made stock). Boil fairly rapidly for 15 minutes, until the potatoes are cooked. Liquidize and return to the pan to keep hot, season with pepper and salt, pour into a large serving bowl and stir in the cream. Serve with croûtons made in butter.

Cow Parsley or **Wild Chervil** *Anthriscus sylvestris* L. Cow parsley is by far the commonest of the early flowering umbellifers in the southern half of England. It is generally distributed and often extremely abundant throughout the British Isles, but infrequent in the northern highlands. It is biennial and occurs by hedgerows, at edges of woods and in waste places. It flowers from April to June.

Cow parsley can be confused with many poisonous species, particularly fool's parsley and hemlock. Pick it as soon as the stems are sufficiently developed for positive identification.

Cow parsley is best used as a herb for garnishing. It has a mild flavour rather like garden chervil *Anthriscus cerefolium* to which it is closely related. Use it on salads, cold potatoes or as a garnish for soups. It is not worthwhile as a cooked herb because it loses its flavour too quickly.

Common Scurvy Grass *Cochlearia officinalis* L. ssp. *officinalis*. Scurvy grass is a biennial or perennial plant, widely distributed throughout the British Isles but infrequent in central southern England and central Ireland. It occurs on drier salt and brackish marshes and on cliffs and banks by the sea; there are also some inland populations. It flowers from May to August.

The use of scurvy grass to cure vitamin C deficiency is of ancient origin. John Gerard, the 16th-century herbalist, tells us that it was 'this excellent plant Caesar's soldiers found to prevail against that plague and hurtfull disease of the teeth, gums, and sinewes'. Captain Cook was the first in this country to advertise the 'wondrous effect' of the herb and it was carried on board ship in the form of dried bundles or the distilled extract.

I dislike the taste of scurvy grass, but long leaved scurvy grass *Cochlearia anglica* is a much more palatable plant.

Cleavers *Galium aparine* L. An annual herb, abundant throughout the British Isles excepting the northern highlands, which occurs in hedges and waste places.

The plant should be used before the hard, round seeds appear. The leaves are stripped from the stem and eaten in soups or as a vegetable.

21

Hedge garlic has a pleasant, oniony flavour that is not too strong and makes a good addition to salads. Photographed April 1.

Hedge Garlic or **Garlic Mustard** *Alliaria petiolata* (Bieb.) Cavara & Grande. A biennial herb, common in Great Britain northwards to Ross and less frequent in Ireland and the Channel Isles, which occurs in hedgerows, wood margins and shady gardens. It flowers from April to June. The leaves can sometimes be seen as early as February if there has been a mild winter and if a warm autumn follows there is often a second crop of stubby, flowerless shoots in September and October. Pick the upper leaves and shoots in March or April when the flowers are in bud.

Hedge garlic was once a very common salad and flavouring herb. In 1657, William Coles wrote in *Adam in Eden, or Nature's Paradise* that it was eaten by 'many country people as sauce to their salt-fish', while a 19th-century edition of Culpeper's *Herbal* urges, 'Reader, just try a little in your next salad'. In some parts of Britain it was traditionally served with boiled mutton and in Wales it has been concocted into a sort of fried bubble-and-squeak, served with either bacon or herrings.

Snow Bell or **Three-Cornered Garlic** *Allium triquetrum* L. An introduced bulb that occurs only in the south-west but in those areas it can be quite common. It is traditionally used as a flavouring in broths.

Alexanders *Smyrnium olusatrum* L. This biennial herb, quite common in the south, is generally found near the sea, in hedges, waste places and on cliffs. It flowers from April to June but the young shoots can be picked in winter and early spring.

Alexanders was introduced by the Romans from its native Mediterranean habitat to add its myrrh-like flavour to broths and stews and to be eaten raw in salads. It was also planted as a vegetable in the early monastery gardens and is often found growing prolifically by the ruins of old abbeys and castles in Ireland and the west of England. The 17th-century diarist John Evelyn included it among 'plants for the Kitchen garden', and it continued to be used widely, as a vegetable and for flavouring, until it was displaced by celery.

As a vegetable alexanders are in prime condition just before the flowers actually open. Cut the stems as low as you can, trim into pan-sized lengths and then peel with a knife as you would rhubarb (it is easier to peel if anything). Boil in salted water for about 6-8 minutes until completely tender, then serve piping hot with ground black pepper and butter, using one or two of the young leaves to decorate. Any left-over leaves are lovely in salads.

'Alisander Butter'd or Fry'd
First parboil them and get the skin off, then boil them in their lengths very tender, and make a Batter with Rhenish Wine, Eggs and Flour, and then dip them in and sauce them with melted Butter, Sack and Sugar; you may do them savoury.'
Les Plantes Médicinales by Dr Losch, 1907, Paris.

Alexanders Sauce

35 g (1½ oz) butter
35 g (1½ oz) flour
6 dl (1 pint) milk, salt and pepper to taste
1 tablespoon chopped alexanders leaves

Knead the butter and flour or work them together with a fork or spoon until they are quite smoothly mixed. Heat the milk and, when just below boiling point, gradually whisk in the butter and flour mixture and continue until the sauce comes to the boil, by which time all the thickening must be smoothly blended into the whole. Add the chopped alexanders and the seasoning and stir.

Wild Garlic or **Ramsoms** *Allium ursinum* L. It is a native bulb, rather common throughout the British Isles in damp woods and lanes. The fresh young leaves can be used in salads or added to soups and stews as a flavouring.

Three-cornered garlic. The leaves can be used for flavouring but only pick them if you find them in abundance. Photographed April 12.

Wild garlic. It has a very strong flavour. Photographed April 10.

Alexanders make a most exciting vegetable served as you would asparagus. Photographed near Looe in Cornwall, March 30.

Crystallized flowers are very delicate and decorative but do not pick flowers of any plant that is in short supply. Photographed April 10.

Violet *Viola odorata* L. Violet is taken from the Latin form of the Greek name Ione. This springs from the legend that when Jupiter changed his beloved Io into a white heifer for fear of Juno's jealousy, he caused these modest flowers to grow to provide fitting food for her. Another legend says that violets sprung from the blood of Ajax:

> *And when stern Ajax poured a purple flood,*
> *The Violet rose, fair daughter of his blood.*

When Napoleon was imprisoned in Elba he promised to return with the violets in the spring and thus the violet became the symbol of the French underground movement at that time. Autumn blooming of violets is said to foretell a deadly epidemic. To dream of violets means an improvement in fortune, while a wreath of violets worn round the neck will prevent drunkenness. A wine made from violet flowers was much used by the Romans, while the Egyptians and Turks valued its use in a sorbet.

Primrose *Primula vulgaris* Huds. Primroses tend to have ominous associations because in the past they were much sought after to strew on graves and dress corpses. It was thought dangerous to bring fewer than 13 into the house.

The leaves of the primrose may be eaten as a salad or boiled as a green pot-herb. The flowers may be fermented to form an intoxicating wine or ground with rice, almonds, honey and saffron to form a 'primrose pottage'. Primrose tea may be used to cure the 'phrensie'.

Crystallized Violets or Primroses

Beat up an egg white with a little rose-water then coat the flowers with the mixture, using a soft brush. Dip them in castor sugar and leave overnight to dry off. Although these crystallized flowers are straightforward to make I think it is a shame to pick them unless you find them in abundance.

'Flowers candied as they grow' – a traditional recipe. 'Make gum-water as strong as for Inke, but make it with Rose-water; then wet any growing flower therewith, about ten of the clock in a hot Summers day, and when the Sun shineth bright, bending the flowers so as you may dip it all over therein, and then shake the flower well; or else you may wet the flower with a soft callaver pensil, then strew the fine searced powder of double refined sugar upon it: Do this with a little box of Searce, whose bottom consisteth of an open lawn, and having also a cover on the top, holding a paper under each flower, to receive the sugar that falleth by: and in three hours it will candy, or harden upon it; and so you may bid your friends after dinner to a growing banquet: or else you

Violets, whilst they make lovely crystallized cake decorations, are even prettier in the hedgerow. Photographed April 1.

Primroses. Photographed April 1.

Lamb's lettuce or corn salad can be found on roadsides, in old gardens and on arable land. Photographed March 28.

may cut off these flowers so prepared, and dry them after in dishes two or three dayes in the sun, or by a fire, or in a stove; and so they will last six or eight weeks, happily longer, if they be kept in a place where the gum may not relent. You may do this also in Balme, Sage, or Borrage, as they grow.'

The Garden of Eden by Sir Hugh Plat, 1659. (I presume that gum-water is made with white of egg.)

Wild rose petals can be used for jam, ice-cream or syrup. Photographed May 1.

Lamb's Lettuce or **Corn Salad** *Valerianella locusta* (L.) Laterrade. Lamb's lettuce or corn salad occurs fairly commonly all over the British Isles on roadsides, arable land and as a garden weed, sometimes on walls. It is much better known on the Continent and has long been a favourite salad plant in France under the names 'Mache', 'Doucette', 'Salade de Chanoine' and 'Salade de Prêtre', the latter referring to the frequency with which it is eaten during Lent. The young leaves are gathered in spring and autumn and eaten as a salad with French or other dressing.

Lamb's Lettuce Salad

This is a delicious salad herb with a tangy sharpness like *radichio*. The dressing should be a rather tart French dressing, with plenty of lemon to bring out the refreshing taste. A super addition is a peeled and sliced grapefruit or orange.

Corn Salad Soup

Wash a quantity of corn salad and half as much again of chervil. Chop and put them in a saucepan with a third more cold water than required of liquid when the soup is ready. Let this boil with the lid on the pan until a third of the water has evaporated. Towards the end add salt, pepper and a good-sized piece of butter.

The Kitchen Companion by Viconte de Mauduit, 1939.

Coltsfoot flowers for wine making can often be found in great quantities on old gravel pits. Photographed April 18.

Gorse bushes daub the dull hillsides with bright, chrome yellow and they make a lovely wine. Photographed April 22.

Coltsfoot *Tussilago farfara* L. A perennial herb abundant throughout the British Isles, it is found especially on waste places, gravel pits, banks, landslides, boulder-clay cliffs and also on dunes and screes. It flowers from March to April, before the leaves appear.

The dried leaves of coltsfoot were formerly smoked as a remedy for asthma and coughs.

Coltsfoot Wine

3 litres (5 pints) coltsfoot flowers
1 kg (2.2 lb) sugar
4½ litres (1 gallon) water
Juice of 2 lemons
General purpose yeast

Traditionally, this wine was made from the petals only, but I have found that to cut away the stem and some of the outer green calyx with a pair of scissors is quicker and does not adversely affect the flavour of the wine.

Prepare the coltsfoot flowers and place them in a plastic bucket. Pour 2 litres (3 pints) of boiling water on the flowers and leave them to soak for 24 hours, pressing them occasionally with a wooden spoon. Then, strain off the flowers through muslin, squeezing hard at the end to extract all the flavour. Add the juice of the lemons and put the yeast to start. Boil the sugar in 2 litres (3 pints) of water to dissolve it and add it to the bucket. When the liquid has cooled, add the yeast, cover and leave to ferment for three days, then transfer to a fermentation jar. Make up the quantity with rest of the cold boiled water and seal with an airlock. Leave in a warm place 16-20°C (60-70°F) until fermentation has ceased. Then siphon the wine into a clear jar, leaving the main sediment behind. Seal with a cork and leave for a month. Filter the wine to get a sparkling result but if you prefer not to filter it, leave in the jar until the sediment has all settled out and then siphon it off. Bottle and cork with sterilized corks.

Gorse *Ulex europaeus* L. Gorse is generally distributed throughout the British Isles, although it is often planted in northern Scotland and, rather infrequently, in west Ireland. It occurs in rough, grassy places and edges of heaths, usually on the lighter and less calcareous soils, and flowers from March to June.

The English name derives from the Anglo-Saxon 'gorst', a waste, a reference to the open moorland on which it is found. Gorse was burned at Midsummer and blazing branches were carried round the herd to bring health to the cows for the coming year. Tradition asserts that gorse brews one of the best wines, while in earlier times the flowers were used to flavour whisky.

Gorse Flower Wine

2 litres (3.5 pints) gorse flowers
1 kg (2.2 lb) sugar
2 lemons
2 oranges
4½ litres (1 gallon) water
General purpose yeast

Pick nice fresh flowers that have come out fully. Thick gardening gloves or tweezers will keep down the wear and tear on your fingers. Start the yeast. Simmer the flowers in the water for 15 minutes then dissolve the sugar, pour into a bucket and add the juice of the lemons and oranges plus the thinly peeled rind. Allow to cool to blood heat, add the yeast and let it stand with a cloth over it. After 3 days, strain off the solids and pour into a fermentation jar, fit an airlock and allow it to ferment until it is finished. Rack off into a clean jar making it up to the full amount with cold boiled water. Leave for a month and then filter or alternatively leave until completely clear then bottle in sterilized bottles.

I got this recipe from Frank Duke and Honor in Cawsand. They normally use 1.4 kg (3 lb) of sugar which gives a medium sweet wine but I prefer to cut the quantity a bit and sweeten it at the bottling stage if it is too dry. An interesting variation is to add 50 g (2 oz) of root ginger to the flowers at the simmering stage.

Gorse Flower Tea

Put 2 tablespoons of freshly picked gorse flowers in a mug of boiling water. Bruise the flowers before adding the water and infuse for 7 to 10 minutes, then strain. The tea can be sweetened with honey if desired. If the flowers are dried, use only 1 tablespoon per mug of water.

Cowslip – too rare to pick. Photographed April 29.

Golden Saxifrage *Chrysosplenium oppositifolium* L. This is found in wet places, stream sides, wet rocks and in woods throughout the British Isles. It is pleasant to eat as a lightly boiled vegetable, flavoured with a little pepper, but only pick if you know a site where it grows in profusion.

Lady's Smock *Cardamine pratensis* L. It occurs commonly in damp meadows and near streams. The leaves have a hot, strong flavour like watercress so are useful to flavour sandwiches or salads. I hesitate to pick this plant as the light pink flowers are so lovely in the dark, wet meadows.

Cowslip *Primula veris* L. This is found on roadsides, hills and pastures, especially on calcareous soils, and it flowers from April to June. In the past, cowslip wine was a great favourite in country districts but I feel that of all the wild flower wines this is the one that I am most opposed to making because there has been a serious decline in the cowslip population during this century. Recently, they do seem to be on the increase again but this wine requires such a large quantity of flowers that I feel it is best to avoid making it if possible.

Sea Kale *Crambe maritima* L. Sea kale is a native perennial occuring from Fife and Islay southwards and in Ireland. It is found on coastal sands, shingle, rock and cliffs and is often a plant of the driftline. It flowers from June to August. Sea kale was known to the Romans who gathered it from the wild and preserved it in barrels for use during long voyages. Inhabitants of coastal regions commonly picked it for use as a cabbage-like vegetable, while later it was cultivated in a blanched form in gardens so that the stalks could be eaten and sold in the markets of England and France.

To Blanch Sea Kale

This is really for those who live near the sea. During March, as the sea kale puts out its first leaves, cover the total plant so that no light can get to it. This is easier than it sounds as sea kale is usually found in deep shingle. In two weeks if the weather is mild, and if you can find your hidden plant again, you will be able to unearth or unshingle it and collect the long white leaf stems with tiny leaf ends.

Jane Grigson, in her *Vegetable Book*, bewails the failure of the British to make the most of what she refers to as the 'English contribution to the basic treasury of best vegetables'.

Steamed Blanched Sea Kale

Trim and clean the blanched leaf stalks carefully, making sure to get out all the sand and grit. Tie the stalks in small bunches and simmer gently in a sealed pan, with only a little water, for about 20 minutes. Serve with a sauce of melted butter and lemon juice or a hollandaise sauce.

Baked Blanched Sea Kale

Place four or five stalks of blanched sea kale for each person in an open oven-proof dish, cover with a cheese sauce made with English Cheddar and then add a sprinkling of Parmesan. Bake in a medium oven for 40 minutes.

As a Vegetable

The best and most succulent part of the unblanched sea kale are the young flower heads before they come out. Cut away any stem which is at all tough, boil in salted water for about 5 minutes so that they are cooked but still a bit crunchy, and serve with freshly ground black pepper and butter.

Lady's smock. Photographed April 20

Sea kale growing straight out of Chesil Beach pebbles. Photographed April 19.

Blanched sea kale lightly boiled and served in the traditional manner on a napkin. Photographed April 23.

Easter-ledge pudding. Photographed on the fell near Grassmere, April 18.

Bistort or **Easter-Ledge** *Polygonum bistorta* L. Bistort is found scattered throughout the British Isles but is rare in the south-east and Ireland. It is common only in west and north-west England. Bistort grows in meadows and grassy roadsides and is commoner on siliceous soils, often forming large patches. It is perennial and flowers from June to August.

The specific name of this plant, and the common English name, comes form the Latin *bis,* meaning twice, and *torta,* twisted, referring to the nature of the rootstock. The plant is also known as Passion Dock. The plant contains a great deal of tannin and was formerly believed to protect against infectious diseases. John Hill, in the 18th-century, says, 'If we minded our own Herbs, we should need fewer medicines from abroad. The Root of Bistort is one of the best Astringents in the world: Not violent but sure'.

Bistort is traditionally eaten at Easter and another country name, Easter Giant, is a corruption of Easter-mangient, meaning a plant to be eaten at that time. A common dish was Easter-Ledge Pudding, with bistort as the principal ingredient. In the north of England, where the plant is commonest, an annual contest is held to find the best bistort pudding.

The leaves and young shoots of bistort may also be boiled and eaten as a green vegetable and the roots, which contain much starch, become edible after steeping in water and then roasting. Thus prepared, the roots have been commonly consumed in Russia, Siberia and Iceland in times of scarcity.

Easter-Ledge Pudding
From Mrs Scott of Wigton, Cumberland, from her great-great-grandmother, and taken from Theodora Fitzgibbon's *A Taste of the Lake District*.

Bistort leaves as you find them at Easter. Photographed April 18.

SERVES FOUR
450 g (1 lb) young bistorts and young nettle tops
1 large onion
125 g (4 oz) pot barley
1 egg
A large knob of butter
½ teaspoon salt, pepper

Chop the greens and onion finely and sprinkle the washed barley among them, adding the salt. Boil in a muslin bag for about 2 hours. Before serving, beat the mixture in a dish with 1 egg, a large knob of butter, salt and pepper (some people mix in a cup of oatmeal at this stage), then make into a cake and fry in fat. Eat with bacon and eggs or fried potatoes. Chopped hard-boiled egg can also be added and in some parts of Cumberland, dandelion or lady's mantle *(Alchemilla vulgaris)* is added as well. This dish is reputed to be a very good spring tonic.

Bistort in flower. They are easier to find at this stage. Photographed June 27.

Sorrel, traditionally one of the most widely used plants, used here to make a delectable soup. Photographed at Denham Lock, May 1.

Sorrel *Rumex acetosa* L. A perennial herb, generally distributed and common throughout the British Isles, it occurs on grassland, including roadside banks, in open places in woods, and is generally found where the soil contains iron. It flowers from May to August but the leaves can be picked as early as February.

Sorrel has been employed from the most distant times as a salad. It was extensively cultivated in Britain until Henry VIII's reign when it was ousted by the large-leaved French sorrel *(R. scutatus)*. John Pechy, 1694, tells us 'the Juice may be mix'd with Broths, or the Leaves boyl'd in them. In Summer 'tis good sauce for most eats.' Traditionally, it was used in country districts as a green sauce

with cold meats. The plants were ground down in a mortar and the resulting purée mixed with vinegar and sugar in the manner of a mint sauce.

In France, sorrel is put into ragouts, fricassees and soups and forms the chief constituent of the favourite soup *aux herbes*. The name sorrel comes from the Old French *surele*, derived from *sur* meaning sour, referring to the characteristic acidity of the plant. The juice of the leaves will curdle milk and is used by the Laplanders as a substitute for rennet. In England, children eat leaves of sorrel on the way to school; they are known as 'sour dabs'.

When cooking, stainless steel knives and non-stick saucepans

Sorrel sauce served on fresh poached salmon. Photographed April 14.

should not be used as the plant chemicals react with iron. Sorrel should not be eaten continually as it contains small amounts of oxalic acid, but a good soup of it occasionally will do you no harm.

Sorrel Soup

SERVES FOUR
Large handful of sorrel leaves, washed and broken into pieces
1 small lettuce (or a few trimmings), washed and broken into pieces
1 large onion, chopped
12 g (½ oz) butter
1 large potato
1 litre (1½ pints) chicken stock (or stock cube and water)
3 dl (½ pint) milk
Salt and pepper

Melt the butter in a large saucepan, add the leaves and onion and soften without browning. Add the potato and boiling stock. Simmer uncovered for 20-30 minutes until the potato is cooked. Sieve or liquidize for a few seconds. Add the milk and seasoning. Heat through and serve with fried croûtons. An egg yolk beaten and added at the last minute makes a richer soup. I have used chickweed in place of lettuce.
A Fenland Village Cookery Book by Liz Roman, 1977.

Sorrel Salad

SERVES FOUR
1 small lettuce
1 bunch sorrel leaves
½ clove garlic
Mixed herbs
Black pepper
Salt
2 tablespoons olive oil

Wash the lettuce and the sorrel, shake well and carefully pat dry. Tear into bite-sized pieces and place in a bowl. Put a teaspoon of salt in the bottom of a large wooden salad bowl. Add to this the crushed garlic, a sprinkling of finely chopped mixed herbs and then the salad greens. Sprinkle with the olive oil and toss gently until all the leaves are coated, then grind black pepper over to taste.

This makes a lovely, sharp, tangy salad. The bitter taste of the sorrel is the reason you put no vinegar or lemon in the dressing.

Buttered Sorrel

After washing the sorrel and removing the stalks, put it into pan with only the water clinging to it. Cover closely and simmer for 10 minutes. Strain in a colander, pressing the mixture well with a saucer to remove as much water as possible. Return to the pan, add a good knob of butter, season well with salt and pepper and toss

sorrel over low heat until every leaf is coated with butter. Serve very hot. Allow a large quantity of raw sorrel per person as it boils down considerably. This makes a most interesting vegetable with a tart flavour, like unsweetened rhubarb.

Sorrel being such a traditional dish there are many recipes in the old herbals. Here are two for anyone who wants to have a real go at medieval cookery.

An Herbe Tart

'Take sorrel, spinage, parsely, and boile them in water till they be very soft as pap; then take them up, and presse the water cleane from them, then take good store of yelks of egs boild very hard, and chopping them with the hearbs exceeding small, then put in good store of currants, sugar and cynamon, and stirre all well together; then put them into a deep tart-coffin with good store of sweet butter, and cover it, and bake it like a pippin-tart, and adorne the lid after the baking in that manner also, and so serve it up.'

Pippin Tart

'Bake it according to the manner of Tarts; and when it is bak't, then draw it out, and having boyld butter and rose-water together, anoynt all the lid over therewith, and then scrape or strow on it good store of sugar, and so set it in the oven again, and after serve it up.'

Both these recipes are from *Country Contentments or the English Huswife* by Gervase Markham, 1623.

Sorrel Soop with Eggs

'Your stock must be made with a Knucle of Veal and a Neck of Mutton, well skim'd and clean; put in a Faggot of Herbs; season with Pepper, Salt, Cloves and Mace, and when it is well boiled and tender strain all off; then let it settle a little, and skim all the Fat off; then take your Sorrel and chop it, but not small, and pass it in brown Butter; put in your Broth and some slices of French Bread; stove in the Middle a Fowl, or a Piece of a Neck of Mutton; then garnish your Dish with Slices of fry'd Bread and some stewed Sorrel, and poach six Eggs, and lay round the Dish, or in your Soop; so serve away hot.'

Sorrel with Eggs

'Your Sorrel must be quick boil'd and well strained; then poach three Eggs soft and three hard; butter your Sorrel well, fry some Sippets and lay three poach'd Eggs and three whole hard Eggs betwixt, and stick Sippets all over the Top, and garnish with slic'd Orange and curl'd Bacon or Ham fry'd.'

Both these recipes are from *The Compleat City and Country Cook* by Charles Carter, 1736.

Sorrel Sauce

125 g (4 oz) sorrel leaves
2 chopped shallots or heaped tablespoons chopped onion
2 tablespoons vermouth (bianco or dry white)
4 tablespoons dry white wine
3 large egg yolks
225 g (8 oz) lightly salted butter

Strip sorrel off the stems, wash, and cut the leaves into small strips. Boil shallots/onions with the wines and 4 tablespoons of water, until liquid has almost vanished. Put the onions with the yolks into a blender and whizz at top speed for 30 seconds. Return to the pan. Cut up the butter and melt with half the sorrel leaves. When almost boiling, remove from heat, pour onto yolks very slowly, stirring vigorously, then increase the speed as sauce thickens. Taste and gradually add the rest of the sorrel. Reheat sauce over a gentle heat or in a bain-marie. Do not over-heat as eggs and butter may curdle. Serve with poached salmon, salmon trout or sea bass.

This recipe is reproduced by permission of Jane Grigson and was first published in the *Observer* Magazine.

Dandelion wine has a fine, sharp flavour with just a hint of resin, like a mild Retsina.

Photographed in Woodchester, April 21.

Dandelion *Taraxacum officinale* Weber. A perennial herb, abundant throughout the British Isles, which occurs in pastures, meadows, lawns, waysides and wasteplaces. The dandelion flowers profusely in April and the leaves can be found at any time of the year except the very coldest months.

The name dandelion is derived from the French *Dent-de-lion* referring to the toothed edges of the leaves or, possibly, to the white pointed roots. Therapeutic use of the dandelion was first recorded by the Arabian physician and herbalist, Avicenna, in the tenth century, and in the thirteenth century it occurs in the Welsh herbal of the physicians of Mydrai. The dandelion has been used as a food plant in many regions. In Minorca the islanders subsisted on it when a swarm of locusts destroyed other vegetation. John Evelyn, the 17th-century diarist, tells us that 'With this homely salley, Hecate entertained Theseus'; and in wartime England Charles Hill, the Radio Doctor, recommended the leaves as a food.

The young leaves are often eaten as a salad on the Continent, especially in France, but the full-grown leaves are too bitter to be used. If the leaves are left to stand in water overnight this will greatly improve them, as it does all wild salad plants. The young leaves are also served as a vegetable, cooked as spinach, or as a vegetable soup, and the flowers are fermented to make wine. Dandelion roots may also be used in salads, grated or chopped – the two-year-old roots are best – but the roots are more frequently roasted and used as coffee. Dandelion beer is a rustic, fermented drink, common at one time in many parts of the country and also in Canada. In the Midlands, dandelion stout was a favourite of the many herb beers brewed in the industrial towns. Dandelions were also fermented in combination with nettles and yellow dock.

In the past, dandelions were cultivated in kitchen gardens where they sometimes attained a huge size. The leaves can be blanched by covering with flower pots and may be induced to last through the winter by removing the flower buds as they appear. In France, dandelions can still be bought in the markets under the name, *pissenlit*.

Pick the young leaves in spring or through the rest of the year, choosing the youngest leaves from the heart of the plant. Strip the leaves from the plant by hand, trim off the excess stalk and wash well. If you want to avoid staining your hands brown, wear gloves!

Dandelion Flower Wine

MEDIUM DRY
Makes 4½ litres (1 gallon)
1 litre (1½-2 pints) dandelion flowers
1 kg (2.2 lb) bag of sugar
2 oranges
2 teaspoons dried yeast
2 litres (½ gallon) boiling water
Extra boiling water needed for topping up jar

Pick the dandelions on a sunny day and press flowers down lightly as you fill the pot. Cut off any green stalks that may be left on. Put the flowers into a bucket and pour on boiling water. You may use two campden tablets if you wish. Now leave for two or three days then strain through wine bag into a gallon jar. Make up sugar syrup with the bag of sugar and start yeast to ferment. Allow sugar syrup to cool to blood heat before putting in the yeast. Grate rind and squeeze juice of oranges into a 4 litre (1 gallon) jar and make up amount with cooled, boiled water. Seal the jar with an airlock and leave until fermentation has finished. Syphon into a clean jar and leave for as long as possible as it improves with keeping.

From Jenny Stone.

This recipe makes a wine with a slightly resinous flavour, a taste which grows on you. I also tried it cutting the green ends (calyxes) off each flower with a pair of scissors. This reduces the resinous taste.

35

Pissenlit served with bacon and croûtons. Photographed April 2.

Salade de Pissenlit

A little salad, or side salad to be served with a rich meat dish, can be made from young and tender dandelion leaves (or leaves that have been blanched), with a light dressing of olive oil and a squeeze of lemon juice. This is garnished with a sprinkling of finely chopped chives, parsley, garlic or borage. A popular French salad which is delicious when served, as in their sophisticated restaurants, as *Pissenlit au Lard.* Make by trimming blanched pickled pork or bacon, then cut it into small pieces and fry until crisp and dry and serve them at once on the raw dandelion salad on a piping-hot plate, with a light dressing made of vinegar, a little oil or bacon fat and a seasoning of salt and pepper. ·

Reproduced from *How to Enjoy your Weeds* by Audrey Wynne Hatfield, by permission of the publishers Frederick Muller Ltd.

I made it by using bacon and croûtons fried in the bacon fat. I also tried it with a little wild chervil.

Dandelion Flower Wine – an older version

Here is a recipe from Harry Westbury whose family lived for three generations at Compton Scorpion Manor, part of Sir Thomas Beecham's estate in Warwickshire. The recipe was passed down to him by his grandmother Mrs David Westbury.

3 litres (6 pints) dandelion flowers
1¼ kg (3 lb) sugar
1 orange
1 lemon
4½ litres (1 gallon) water
General purpose yeast

36

Peel the orange and lemon (with as little pith as possible). Put the peel and the dandelion heads into a muslin bag and boil in the water for 20 minutes. Remove the bag, squeeze lightly and dissolve the sugar in the remaining liquid. Put into a bucket (not metal) and when lukewarm (not *cold*) add the juice of the orange and lemon and mix the yeast with a little of the liquid and pour back into the bucket.

Leave to work for 3 days, then syphon into a fermentation jar and leave until it has finished fermenting. When fermentation is quite finished bottle it up. The longer the wine is kept the better it tastes.

Dandelion Beer

Apart from being a very popular country tipple, dandelion beer was the drink most favoured in the past by workers in iron foundries and potteries. It is refreshing and particularly good for relieving stomach upsets or indigestion and for clearing the kidneys and bladder. The whole plants are grubbed up to make it and the following recipe is worth the making in springtime:

225 g (½ lb) young dandelion plants
1 lemon
4½ litres (1 gallon) water
12 g (½ oz) root ginger
25 g (1 oz) yeast
450 g (1 lb) demerara sugar
25 g (1 oz) cream of tartar

Wash the plants and remove the hairy roots without breaking the main tap roots. Put them into a pan with the bruised ginger root, the lemon rind (no white pith) and the water. Boil for 10 minutes, then strain out the solids and pour the liquid over the sugar and cream of tartar in the fermenting vessel. Stir until the sugar is dissolved. When the liquid is lukewarm, add the yeast and the lemon juice and leave the vessel, covered with a folded cloth, in a warm room for five days. Strain out all the sediment and bottle in screw-topped cider or beer bottles. This beer is ready to drink in about a week, when it hisses as the stopper is loosened. It does not keep very long.

From *How to Enjoy Your Weeds* by Audrey Wynne Hatfield, by permission of the publishers Frederick Muller Ltd.

Test the bottles daily to see that they don't get too fizzy. Even after only two days in the bottles it is smashing.

To blanch, cut away the dandelion leaves and allow the new leaves to grow in the complete dark under a plastic bag or in an old bucket. This way they will be much less bitter. Photographed May 25.

Ground ivy is common all over the British Isles except the far north. Photographed May 12.

Ground Ivy *Glechoma hederacea* L. Ground ivy was one of the principal plants used by the early Saxons to clarify their beers. It improved the flavour and keeping qualities of the beer and rendered it clearer. For this reason it was known as ale-hoof and the beer was called gill-ale after another English name for the plant. Ground ivy continued in general use until the reign of Henry VIII when hops were introduced. It was also a constituent of local importance at Ludlow during Easter, when it was used as a stuffing for leg of pork. In the autumn hairy tumours may be seen on the leaves formed by a species of gall wasp. These tumours have a strong flavour of the plant and were eaten by the peasantry of France. Ground ivy should be gathered during spring and early summer. It has a very strong, bitter taste, only suitable as an additive to a beer or salad to sharpen the taste.

Boiled Dandelion

Wash the leaves thoroughly in the same manner as is done for spinach, so as to rid them all of sand or earth, and let them stand in cold water for a couple of hours. Drain, throw into boiling water with a little salt, and let them boil for 20 minutes, press out the water and serve with melted butter.

Recipes for the Million, 1897.

Dandelion Coffee

The root should be dug from September to March. Drinking Chocolate is sometimes mixed with the coffee to improve the flavour. For a detailed recipe on dandelion coffee, see page 154.

Dandelion Nitsuke

Pick dandelions while the leaves are still tender and before the flowers bloom.

225 g (½ lb) dandelion greens
1 tablespoon sesame oil
3 tablespoons shoyu or 1 tablespoon miso, thinned with 2 tablespoons water
1 tablespoon white sesame seeds, toasted and chopped

Wash the greens well and chop them finely. Heat the oil in a heavy skillet, add the chopped greens and sauté over medium heat for 2 or 3 minutes. Season with shoyu or thinned miso and simmer until dry. Serve sprinkled with chopped sesame seeds.

Variation: To prepare dandelion roots, scrub them well, then mince. Sauté in a little sesame oil over medium heat for 3 or 4 minutes. Season with shoyu or thinned miso and simmer until dry. Use sparingly as a garnish with rice. A traditional remedy for arthritis.

The Art of Just Cooking by Lima Ohsawa, 1974.

Ohitashi Goma-ai

Steam the leaves and mix with roasted sesame seeds that have been seasoned with soy sauce.

The Chico-San Cookbook by Cornellia Aihara, 1972.

A mouthwatering St George's soufflé flan. Photographed April 28.

St George's Mushroom *Tricholoma gambosum* (Fr) Kummer. Occurring on pasture land, wood edges and roadsides, it is traditionally found on St George's Day, April 23, and it is from this that it gets its name, but in most years it will occur a week or two later. It has a strong, mealy smell and taste which is reduced in cooking. Personally I do not like eating the large, older specimens but fresh, young ones are very good. In France its common name is mousseron and it is one of the most searched-for species.

St George's Mushroom

SERVES TWO
300 g (10 oz) St George's mushrooms
50 g (2 oz) butter
1–2 tablespoons yoghurt
A sprinkle of marjoram
A pinch of oregano
A little grated nutmeg

Parsley
Salt and pepper

Sauté the mushrooms, parsley, herbs and seasoning for 5-10 minutes in the butter. Allow the juices to evaporate. Add the yoghurt and simmer for 15-20 minutes until the yoghurt has been absorbed. Do not let it boil or the yoghurt will coagulate.

Jeff and Jenny Stone, who gave me this excellent recipe, suggest serving it with a bean flan or as a starter with toast or croutons.

Soufflé Flan with St George's Mushroom Filling

SERVES FOUR

Souffle Flan:
35 g (1½ oz) butter
50 g (2 oz) flour

3 dl (½ pint) milk
3 eggs, separated
Salt and black pepper

Preheat oven to 200°C (400°F, Mark 6). Butter a 20 cm (8 in) flan
dish and dust with flour.

Melt the butter in a pan, stir in the flour, salt and pepper to make
a smooth paste. Gradually stir in milk. Bring to the boil and cook
for 1 minute, stirring continuously. Beat the egg yolks and add to
the pan a little at a time, mixing continuously. Cook for one more
minute but do not allow to boil. Set aside and allow to cool to room
temperature.

Beat egg whites until stiff and fold into cooled sauce. Pour the
mixture into the prepared flan dish, making sure to spread more
sauce around the edge of the dish. Bake for 25 minutes until it has
risen and browned.

Filling:
25 g (1 oz) butter
100 g (4 oz) St George's mushrooms
½ an onion
Small bunch of cooked, chopped spinach or sea beet
½ teaspoon parsley
100 g (4 oz) curd cheese
2 teaspoons flour
Pinch of nutmeg
Salt and pepper

Sauté mushrooms and chopped onions in the butter for 5 minutes.
Add chopped spinach, parsley, salt, pepper and flour. Cook for
another 2 minutes. Add the curd cheese, sour cream and nutmeg
and blend together. Spoon evenly onto the soufflé leaving the fluffy
edges exposed and return to the oven for 3 minutes so that it is
piping hot when you serve it.

This dish can be made with any kind of mushrooms.

Jew's Ears *Auricularia auricula – judae* St Amans. It can be found
at all times of year in warm, wet spells on old elder branches.

Pechey, 1694, says of this fungus: 'It grows to the Trunk of the
Elder-Tree. Being dried it will keep a good Year. Boyl'd in Milk, or
infus'd in Vinegar, 'tis good to gargle the Mouth or Throat in
Quinsies, and other Inflammations of the Mouth and Throat. And
being infus'd in some proper Water, it is good in Diseases of the
Eyes.'

Because of the host trees, the name is said to be a corruption of
'Judas's ear', from the tradition that Judas hung himself on an
elder. In China, Jew's ears and allied species are much prized as
food. The fungus should be gathered while still soft and cut from
the tree with a knife, then washed well and finely sliced.

Jew's Ear Rolls

SERVES FOUR
225 g (8 oz) Jew's ears
50 g (2 oz) butter
3 or 4 cloves of garlic, finely chopped
A pinch of thyme
Parsley
Salt and pepper
White bread

Wash the Jew's ears well and dry on kitchen towel or paper.
Simmer in the butter with the garlic, thyme, parsley and seasoning.
When tender, after cooking for approximately 20-30 minutes,
spoon onto slices of bread with crusts removed (the much despised,
white sliced bread really works best, but any will do), roll each into
a little sausage and secure with a tooth pick. Put on dish and brown
in the oven or under the grill, first dotting with butter.

From Elizabeth Smart of Bungay.

This is a most successful recipe.

St George's mushrooms cooked with yoghurt and herbs. Photographed April 31.

Jew's ears can be found on old elder branches. Photographed May 5.

Hop top omelette, a really worthwhile dish. Photographed May 1.

Hop *Humulus lupulus* L. This perennial climber is widely distributed but probably because it has often escaped from cultivation. The hop occurs in hedges and thickets and flowers in July and August.

The hop is first mentioned by Pliny as a garden plant of the Romans who used only the young shoots, in spring, as a vegetable. Formerly, it was sold in markets, tied in bundles, for table use. The shoots can also be eaten raw in salads and the early foliage may be used as a pot-herb.

The generic name is derived from *humus* meaning earth, while *lupulus* is from *lupus*, a wolf, referring to the vine's tendency to choke the plant on which it climbs. The English name is from the Anglo-Saxon, *hoppan*, to climb.

Hop Shoot Omelette

SERVES TWO

This is an Italian style omelette cooked in olive oil rather than butter and served flat, not turned over:

4 eggs
A handful of hop shoots
Salt and pepper
Olive oil

Lightly beat the eggs and flavour with seasoning. Add the hop tops using only the top 5 cm (2 in). Fry in olive oil until fairly solid, cut in two and serve. This is an unusual dish, ideal for a light lunch.

Hop Top Soup

'Take a large quantity of hop tops, in April, when they are in their greatest perfection; tie them in bunches twenty or thirty in a bunch; lay them in spring-water for an hour or two, drain them well from the water, and put them to some thin pease soup; boil them well, and add three spoonfuls of the juice of onions, some pepper, and salt; let them boil some time longer; when done, soak some crusts of bread in the broth, and lay them in the tureen, then pour in the soup.'

The Lady's Assistant by Mrs Charlotte Mason (First published 1775, a new edition 1786)

I made my version of this soup by sautéing an onion in butter then adding 1 litre (2 pints) of chicken stock, a tin of peas, a large handful of hop tops and cooking gently for half an hour. When flavouring it, I used a touch of cayenne pepper and served it with large croûtons.

Buttered Hop Tops

Gather the young shoots (not later than May), only about four leaves down, and lay to soak in cold water with a handful of salt. Drain, plunge into enough boiling water to cover easily, and boil rapidly until tender. Drain the water off instantly, chop up in the hot pan with pepper, salt and a lump of butter, then serve hot.

Metheglin – an ancient recipe

'Take one Measure of Honey, and three Measures of Water, and let it boil till one measure be boiled away, so that there be left three measures in all; as for Example, take to one Pot of Honey, three Pots of Water, and let it boil so long, till it comes to Three Pots. During which time you must skim it very well as soon as any scum riseth; which you are to continue till there rise no scum more. You may, if you please, put to it some spice, to wit, Cloves and Ginger; the quantity of which is to be proportioned according as you will have your Meath, strong, or weak. But this you do before it begin to boil. There are some that put either Yeast of Beer, or leaven of bread into it, to make it work. But this is not necessary at all; and much less to set it into the sun. Mr Masillon doth neither the one nor the other. Afterwards for to sun it, you must let it grow Luke-warm, for to advance it. And if you do intend to keep your Meathe a long time, you may put into it some hops on this fashion. Take to every Barrel of Meathe a Pound of Hops without leaves, that is, of Ordinary Hops used for Beer, but well cleansed, taking only the Flowers, without the Green leaves and stalks. Boil this pound of Hops in a Pot and half of fair water, till it come to on Pot, and this quantity is sufficient for a Barrel of Meathe. A Barrel at Liege holdeth ninety Pots, and a Pot is as much as a Wine quart in England. (I have since been informed from Liege that a Pot of that Countrey holdeth 48 ounces of Apothecary's measure: which I judge to be a Pottle according to London measure, or two Wine quarts.) When you Tun your Meath, you must not fill your Barrel by half a foot, that so it may have room to work. Then let it stand six weeks slightly stopped; which being expired, if the Meath do not work, stop it up very close. Yet must you not fill up the Barrel to the very brim. After six Months you draw off the clear into another Barrel, or strong Bottles, leaving the dregs, and filling up your new Barrel, or Bottles, and stopping it or them very close.

'The Meath that is made this way, (Viz. In the Spring, in the Month of April or May, which is the proper time for making of it,) will keep many a year.'

Sir Keneleme Digbie, 1669.

Sweet cicely *Myrrhis odorata* (L.) Scop. Sweet Cicely is a perennial, common in northern England and southern Scotland, becoming rarer northwards. In Ireland it is rare except in the north-east. It is found in grassy places, hedges, roadsides and woods and flowers in May and June.

The Latin names are derived from the Greek word for perfume, because of the myrrh-like smell of the plant. All parts of the plant can be used. The aromatic leaves may be used as a salad herb or boiled in soups and stews. The thick root may be boiled like parsnips, as was the custom in the sixteenth and seventeenth centuries, and eaten with oil and vinegar, when it was said to be 'very good for old people that are dull and without courage; it rejoiceth and comforteth the heart and increaseth their lust and strength'.

The roots could also be eaten in salads. The 'long, black shining seeds' are, according to Robinson, 'of a sharp, sweet and pleasant taste'. They were used extensively for flavouring, chopped up in salads or added to the boiled vegetable. The stems, also, may be eaten boiled. The herb was once used when making Chartreuse and the chopped leaves can be added to cooked gooseberries in place of sugar.

Sweet cicely may still be found as an appetizer on more exclusive menus, cooked in batter according to a French recipe.

Sweet cicely. Photographed at Askrigg, Yorkshire, June 10.

Hawthorn and beetroot salad is an incredible colour combination. Photographed May 1.

Hawthorn *Crataegus monogyna* Jacq. This deciduous shrub or small tree occurs throughout the British Isles. It is found in scrub, woods and hedges, dominant on most types of soil, and is the shrub most frequently planted for hedges.

Hawthorn blossom was once the universal expression of delight at the return of summer and was the choice for May Day garlands. Any servant who could bring in a branch of hawthorn blossom on May Day received a dish of cream for breakfast and, in Northamptonshire, a blossoming branch was planted outside the home of the prettiest girl in each village. Unfortunately, since the calendar revisions of 1752, when May Day was brought forward 13 days, the hawthorn is rarely in blossom by this day. Many country villagers believed that the hawthorn flowers still bore the smell of the Great Plague of London and in most counties in England it is thought unlucky to bring it into the house.

Traditionally, a sprig of hawthorn, if gathered on Ascension Day, will protect the house against lightning. The reason for this is given in the rhyme:

> *Under a thorn*
> *Our Saviour was born.*

On May Day, the dew from a hawthorn tree is said to beautify a maid for ever, for which purpose Pepys' wife bathed in hawthorn dew in 1667.

> *The fair maid who the first of May,*
> *Goes to the field at the break of day,*
> *And washes in dew from the hawthorn tree,*
> *Will ever after handsome be.*

The very young leaves of the hawthorn, known as 'Bread and Cheese', are traditionally eaten by children on the way to school. They are best picked in April when they have a pleasantly nutty taste. Hawthorn flower wine was quite common in Britain in former times.

Hawthorn and Beetroot Salad

SERVES TWO
3 dl (½ pint) hawthorn leaves
2 cooked beetroots, diced
French dressing

Wash the hawthorn buds or young leaves and combine with the diced beetroot. Add the French dressing and mix well.

The taste of the hawthorn leaves is very light and delicate.

Hawthorn and Potato Salad

SERVES FOUR
450 g (1 lb) potatoes
6 dl (1 pint) hawthorn buds/leaves
3 tablespoons olive oil
1 tablespoon white wine
2 tablespoons white malt or wine vinegar
Good pinch each of salt and pepper
1 lettuce

Boil the potatoes. If using new potatoes, boil them in their skins then rub off. Dice while still warm and mix with all the ingredients except the hawthorn and lettuce. Mix in hawthorn when cold and serve on bed of lettuce.

Rape *Brassica napus* L. Rape is frequent throughout the British Isles, now increasingly found escaped from cultivation. It may be annual or biennial and is found on roadsides and stream banks near

Rape grown for the seed oil and often found as an escape. Photographed May 4.

Wild cabbage growing on the White Cliffs of Dover. Photographed April 1.

arable land. The flowering period is May to August.

Rape is mainly grown as a seed crop for oil and has been cultivated for this purpose at least since the Middle Ages. It was grown in gardens for winter and spring salads (the younger leaves being used) and it was also cultivated for spring greens, taking the tops first, followed by the side shoots. According to Boorde the roots can also be eaten: 'Rape rootes, if they be well boyled, they do nowrysshe, if they be moderately eaten: immoderately eaten, they doth ingender ventosyte, and doth anoye the stomacke.' By the 19th century rape was being used as autumn forage for sheep.

Although it is generally accepted that rape was an introduced species, it has been suggested that it arose through spontaneous hybridization of *B. campestris* and *B. oleracea*; for example in a medieval garden where turnips and kale grew side by side. The English name derives from the Latin *rapa* – a turnip.

Black Mustard *Brassica nigra* (L.) Koch. Black mustard is an annual found (apparently wild) on cliffs by the sea, especially in south-west England, and on stream-banks throughout England and Wales. However, it is common only as an escape in waysides and waste places. It can be found from May to September.

It is not certain when mustard was first used as a condiment but it is amongst the oldest recorded spices, with Sanskrit records dating back to about 3000 BC and an extensive literature from Greek and Roman times onwards. The plant itself probably originated in Asia Minor where it was developed as a commercial spice. Its success soon spread throughout Europe. According to classical tradition it was made known to man by Aesculapius, the god of medicine, and Ceres, the goddess of seeds. From Egypt it was introduced to the Romans, who steeped the crushed seeds in new wine, known as must, and gave it the name *mustrum ardens*, literally burning must, from the hot taste of the seeds. This Latin name was then contracted to become 'mustard'.

The Romans brought the plant to Britain and its use was continued here by the Anglo-Saxons who used the seeds, either whole or slightly crushed, rather than in a paste. In the 16th and 17th centuries Tewkesbury seems to have been the centre of the mustard trade in Britain. It is mentioned in Shakespeare's Henry IV, and in 1657 the herbalist, Coles, wrote: 'In Gloscershire about Teuxbury they grind Mustard seed and make it up into balls which are brought to London and other remote places as being the best that the world affords'. The balls were made by mixing the crushed seed with honey or vinegar and a little cinnamon. The balls would then keep for some time, and could be mixed with more vinegar, for use as required. This method of preparation continued until the end of the 18th century when a Durham lady invented a method of preparing mustard flour, which has long been known as Durham mustard. Black mustard was used by the Romans as a green vegetable, cooked like spinach, and the young leaves may be eaten in salads. An oil which is expressed from the seeds has been used in medicine and soap-making. The seed pods begin to ripen in August.

Wild Cabbage *Brassica oleracea* L. This can be found in waste places, probably as an escape from cultivation, but on the southern coast, especially near the White Cliffs of Dover, it can be found growing in its wild state.

The cabbage is a really ancient vegetable of cultivation; it was certainly known to the Ancient Greeks, Romans, Celts and Saxons and was much prized for its medicinal properties. It was said to be beneficial in the treatment of worms, ulcers, eczema, carbuncles, bronchial afflictions, lumbago and migraines.

This plant, so in demand by apothecaries in the past, is the parent of all the modern cultivated cabbage forms, from Brussel sprouts to cauliflowers and even kohlrabi. When you find it in the wild, just gather the young leaves and shoots, leaving the plant intact to leaf again. Boil them until tender. The flavour is that of the shop-bought cabbage: no better, no worse!

Comfrey with peanuts is a lovely combination. They are also good fried in batter. Photographed May 1.

Comfrey *Symphytum officinale* L. A perennial herb generally distributed throughout Great Britain, although it is less common in the north and Ireland and probably not native there. Comfrey is found in damp places, especially by rivers and streams, and it flowers from May to October. Only the young leaves should be picked and the flowers can be white, pink or deep purple.

Comfrey has long been known as a valuable plant medicinally, indicated by the specific name 'officinale'. The generic name is derived from the Greek *symphyo*, to unite, and refers to the herb's powers of healing broken bones. The English name 'comfrey' refers to the same property, being a corruption of *con firma*, while an old country name for the plant is 'knit-bone'. Comfrey has been used in wound healing since the Middle Ages, for which purpose it was generally grown.

The leaves when young can be cooked like spinach, as a good green vegetable but they are coarse and bitter when older. They have also been used to flavour cakes and other dishes. The stalks, if blanched, can be cooked and eaten like asparagus, while the roots can be used as a coffee substitute and for this purpose may be combined with dandelion roots.

Mrs Grieve's *Herbal* gives the following alternative names: 'knitbone, knitback, consound, blackwort, bruisewort, slippery root, boneset, yalluc (Saxon), gum plant, consolida, ass ear; the many local names of the plant testify to its long reputation as a culinary herb'. The chief and most important constituent of comfrey root is mucilage which it contains in great abundance, more even than marshmallow. Comfrey leaves are mildly astringent and so are frequently used as an external remedy for strains and bruises or made into poultices for cuts and boils.

Comfrey and Peanut

SERVES FOUR
50 g (2 oz) sunflower oil
100 g (4 oz) onion, peeled and chopped
50 g (2 oz) unsalted peanuts
450 g (1 lb) comfrey leaves, chopped
Salt and pepper

Heat the oil in a pan, add the onion and sauté until lightly brown. Add the peanuts and cook for 2 minutes, then add the comfrey leaves and sauté for about 15 minutes until all liquid has been absorbed. Season well with salt and pepper. Comfrey can also be cooked in the same way as spinach.

Comfrey Fritters

SERVES FOUR
100 g (4 oz) flour
1½ dl (¼ pint) tepid water
Comfrey leaves
1 egg
Pinch of salt, cayenne pepper
Hot fat for frying

Separate the egg-white from the yolk. Sieve the flour and salt into a basin, make a well in the centre and drop in the yolk. Add the water, mixing it in gradually with a wooden spoon, work in the flour and leave to stand. Lastly, whip the egg-white to a stiff froth and fold it in. Pick comfrey leaves with a small amount of stalk, wash and dry well and dip the leaves into the batter. Deep fry in hot fat until golden brown on both sides. Drain on paper towels and serve sprinkled with salt and cayenne pepper.

Comfrey Soup

SERVES FOUR
2 large handfuls young, comfrey leaves
1 medium onion
25 g (1 oz) butter
12 g (½ oz) plain flour
1 litre (1½ pints) chicken stock
Salt and freshly ground pepper
Mixed spice to taste
4 tablespoons natural yoghurt

Wash the comfrey leaves and remove any tough stalks. Peel and finely slice the onion, melt the butter in a heavy pan and fry the

White comfrey. Photographed May 6.

Pink comfrey. Photographed June 28.

Purple comfrey. Photographed June 25.

onions until soft. Stir in the flour and gradually add the stock, allowing the mixture to thicken. Add the comfrey leaves and seasoning, then cover and simmer for 30 minutes. Liquidize the soup, return to the pan and reheat. Taste for flavour. Serve with a spoonful of yoghurt and black pepper.

Butterburr. For a child the gigantic leaves make a wonderful secret world to hide in. Photographed May 1.

Butterburr *Petasites hybridus* (L.) Gaertn., Mey. & Scherb.
Forming large patches of enormous, bright green leaves in damp
places and by stream edges, the flowers come before the leaves at
the end of March.

Traditionally the leaves of butterburr were used to wrap butter
which helped keep it cool. Geoffrey Grigson in his excellent book,
The Englishman's Flora, found and quotes a reference in Gerard,
1633, which I have missed: 'The Leaf is of such a wideness, as that
of itself it is bigger and large inough to keepe a mans head from
raine, and from the heat of the sunne.'

Ground Elder or **Goutweed** *Aegopodium podagraria* L. A
perennial herb, generally distributed throughout the British Isles,
it is found at roadsides, in waste places near buildings and as a
persistent weed in gardens. It flowers from May to August but the

best time to use it is in the spring when the shoots are about 15 cm
(6 in) high.

Ground elder was introduced into Britain by the Romans as a
culinary plant and was cultivated throughout the Middle Ages to
be used as a spinach-like vegetable, as a pot-herb and as a medicinal
plant. In the eighteenth century the Swedish botanist, Linneaus,
described it as a good spring vegetable and it is still used
extensively as a pot-herb in Scandinavia, while in Russia and
Lithuania it is used as a vegetable and in salads.

As a Vegetable

Use the young leaves and leaf stems. Wash well and cook in a
tablespoon of butter and a very little water. Add salt and pepper
and cook gently for about 10 minutes, stirring continuously. When
tender, drain well and toss in butter before serving. This is an
excellent vegetable and eating the leaves is a nice way to keep the
ground elder under control in your garden.

Ground elder was favoured by the Romans as a vegetable. Photographed May 10.

Laver bread served on fried bread by the coast near Pembroke. Photographed 29 April.

Laver *Porphyra umbiliculis* J. G. Agardi. Common around our coasts, growing on rocks and stones especially where the rocks are embedded in sand, this seaweed can be found from March onwards, even on a day when there is only a small tide, as it grows on any level of the tide-covered shore.

There are quite a few species that are very similar, forming large, thin, lobed sheets attached to the rocks by a very small disc. The species vary in colour from brown to purple to greenish but in practice you can mix together any species you find. In fact, sea lettuce is often mixed with laver in making laver bread.

Laver is extremely nutritious because it contains a high proportion of protein, iodine and vitamins B, B_2, A, D and C. It is also excellent for slimmers as it contains few calories.

Laver Bread

Collect a good basket of laver, avoiding the very sandy patches. The cleaner you pick it the less washing you will need to do! Break up the large pieces and wash them thoroughly in cold water then boil steadily for about 4 hours in a large pan, checking every 30 minutes to see it does not boil dry. It is cooked when the sheets have broken up into tiny pieces which make a smooth purée. Alternatively, it can be cooked much more rapidly in a steamer. Drain away any excess liquid and store the puréed 'laver bread' in the fridge. It will keep for about a week.

Ancient Recipe

'Laver is an Herb not common, but very good, and grown only in some Parts of the West of England by the Sea on the Rocks, as Samphire: Take a great deal of this, and squeeze it close in pots, after well wash'd; put to it some Crab Verjuice, and set it in the Oven, and bake it gently till soft; then strain the Verjuice from it, but leave it moist, and put it up, four or six Pounds in a Pot, and head it over with clarify'd Butter, and use it as you think fit.'

The Compleat Practical Cook By Charles Carter, 1730.

Laver growing on the rocks. Photographed May 14.

Bladder wrack is common on the rocky coast. Photographed June 16.

Laver Bread in Carmarthen

Laver bread is sold in many places in South Wales. Raymond Rees, a fishmonger in Carmarthen who sells it, said that the local people don't make oat cakes out of it as tradition has it in books. They heat the mixture for 3 or 4 minutes in a pan and then spread it on fried bread and serve it with bacon. This is an excellent and appetizing way of presenting a food which is very beneficial yet rather unpleasant in texture and appearance.

Chinese Egg and Laver Soup

SERVES FOUR
1 handful of laver
2 eggs
3 large spring onions
6 dl (1 pint) chicken stock
Salt and pepper
1 tablespoon sesame seed oil

Take the dried laver, soak it in cold water for 30 minutes and then cut into pieces roughly 1 cm (½ in) square. Chop the spring onions into pieces 1 cm (½ in) long and beat the eggs thoroughly in a bowl. Make up the stock from a stock cube or, preferably, heat up some stock you have made from chicken pieces and when it comes to the boil add the laver and spring onions. Stir and then add the beaten eggs and sprinkle on some pepper and salt if needed. Serve in a tureen or large bowl with a little sesame seed oil floating on top (it will break up into attractive globules).

This is a really good, thoroughly Chinese dish that is well worth making so remember when you see some laver on the beach, take it home, wash it very well to get rid of all the grit and then dry it. I put it on a grid, balanced 5 cm (2 in) above a radiator, for 2 hours or so and then put it away in a dry place. It will be fine even 6 months or a year later.

Bladder Wrack *Fucus vesiculosus* L. One of our most common seaweeds, it is found growing on rocks between the low and high tide levels. The fronds are branched and usually about 50-100 cm (1½-3 ft) long.

Gather the bladder wrack in the early summer leaving the tough stems behind and using only the fresh plants that are still attached to the rocks. The seaweed can be rapidly dried in the sun or in a warm kitchen, then broken up into small pieces which can be used to add to stews and soups for extra body and nourishment.

Wild flower fritters is a dish which is lovely to watch being prepared as well as eat. Photographed in Shannagary, May 14.

Wild Flower Fritters

SERVES FOUR
100 g (4 oz) plain flour
Pinch of salt
1 egg
1½ dl (¼ pint) milk
Dandelion leaves
Crab apple flowers
Alexanders flowers
Yellow rocket flowers

Sift the flour and salt together. Make a well in the centre of the flour and add the egg and some of the milk. Mix gradually to a stiff consistency, using more milk as required. Beat well, adding the rest of the milk. Leave to stand for about 30 minutes before using. Wash the leaves and flower heads and remove leaves from the flower heads, leaving a little stalk to make a good shape. Dry well. Dip each flower head or leaf into the batter holding it by the spare stem. Deep fry at 220°C (425°F, Mark 7) until golden brown on both sides. Drain on kitchen paper and serve hot. (When hot enough the fat should show signs of hazing. It can be tested by dropping a small spot of batter into the fat. If the temperature is correct the batter will rise to the surface immediately and then begin to colour.)

I like to do a Japanese version of this dish combining only the best shapes of the flowers together and also contrasting the strong flavours of, say, the alexanders with the delicate hint of flavour you get from the apple blossom. Serve with a sauce made from soy sauce and saki mixed.

Hogweed *Heracleum sphodylium* L. Hogweed is a biennial herb, common and generally distributed throughout the British Isles in grassy places, roadsides, by hedges and in woods. It flowers from June until October.

The people of Lithuania, said John Gerard in the 16th century, 'used to make drinks with the decoction of this herb and leven or some other thing made of meale, which is used instead of beare and other ordinaire drinks'. Young succulent stems, after being stripped of their envelope, are occasionally eaten as a salad in the Outer Hebrides. In Russia and Siberia the leaf-stalks are dried in the sun and tied up in close bundles until they acquire a yellow colour. When a sweet substance resembling sugar forms upon

Hogweed shoots will surprise and enchant even the most conservative of your friends. Photographed May 14.

·them, they are eaten as a great delicacy. In Lithuania and Siberia a spirit is distilled from the stalks, either on its own or mixed with bilberries. The young shoots and leaves may be boiled and eaten as a green vegetable and when just sprouting from the ground they resemble asparagus in flavour.

Hogweed Shoots

Those who despise this common plant will no longer do so when they sample its succulence. Take only the very young shoots before the leaf has fully uncurled, wash them in cold water and then cook in a heavy pan without drying the stems. Add a good knob of butter, ground black pepper and salt, then cook until tender (for about 8 minutes). Serve with a little cold butter or fresh lemon juice. This is unequivocally one of the best vegetables I have eaten.

Sea beet quiche. Photographed on the steps at Cawsand, June 2.

Sea Beet *Beta vulgaris* ssp. *maritima* (L.) Thell. This annual or perennial herb occurs on sea shores throughout the British Isles and is common along the coasts of England, Wales and Ireland but is infrequent in Scotland. It flowers from July to September.

This plant is thought to be the ancestor of most, if not all, the cultivated varieties of beet – from beetroot to spinach-beet. The use of beet probably dates from prehistoric times when the leaves were almost certainly used as pot-herbs. The Romans fed it to animals and men and it was taken from Italy to northern Europe by the barbarian invaders. By the 16th century it was widely used for

Making sea beet pancakes on the shore. Photographed June 20.

feeding animals, particularly during the winter. The root has no value as food but the leaves form an excellent green vegetable, picked from May to December and cooked as you would spinach.

Sea Beet Quiche
SERVES FOUR

20 cm (8 in) flan case lined with shortcrust pastry
35 g (1½ oz) butter
35 g (1½ oz) flour
3 dl (½ pint) milk
4 handfuls strong English cheddar
1 egg yolk, well beaten
4 handfuls sea beet
Sea salt, black pepper, mustard powder

Melt the butter in a pan, add flour and milk, cheddar and mustard powder to taste. Stir in the egg yolk. Cook the sea beet in only the water left on the leaves after washing; chop finely before adding to the mixture. Flavour with salt and pepper before pouring into the flan case. Bake in a pre-heated oven (175°C, 375°F, Mark 5) for 25 minutes or until nicely browned.

Sea Beet and Yoghurt Soup
SERVES FOUR

4 large handfuls of sea beet
2 onions sliced finely
4 tablespoons olive oil
5 tablespoons rice, washed
3 dl (generous ½ pint) plain yoghurt
1 tablespoon Greek parsley, chopped finely
Chicken stock
Salt, freshly ground black pepper, a pinch of turmeric

Thoroughly wash the sea beet in cold water and slice roughly. Fry the onion lightly in the olive oil in a heavy, earthenware pot. When it is just coloured, stir in the rice and make sure it is all coated in the oil. Add the sea beet and about 1-1¼ litres (1½-2 pints) chicken stock, season well with salt and pepper, bring to the boil and simmer gently until the rice is tender. When cooked, stir in the yoghurt vigorously and add the turmeric. Make sure it's hot but do not let it boil again or else the yoghurt will curdle. Sprinkle on the parsley and serve very hot.

Two delicious recipes from Kyle Cathie, my editor at Pan.

Pancakes Stuffed with Sea Beet
SERVES FOUR-SIX *(12 small pancakes)*

Filling:
Large bunch sea beet
150 g (6 oz) Cheddar cheese
2 peeled tomatoes
Salt and pepper

Wash the sea beet and pull the leaves from the stems. Cook for 10 minutes in a sealed pan, drain and chop. Grate the cheese. When cool, mix together the sea beet, grated cheese, salt and pepper. Peel the tomatoes and slice. Put the filling ingredients to one side.

Pancakes:
100 g (4 oz) plain flour and pinch of salt
1 egg plus 1 egg yolk
3 dl (½ pint) milk,
melted butter or oil
1 tablespoon salt
50-75 g (2-3 oz) white vegetable fat

Sift the flour and salt into a mixing basin and hollow out the centre. Add the egg, egg yolk and half the milk. Stir the ingredients, using a wooden spoon, and gradually draw in the flour around the sides of the bowl. Beat well to form a smooth batter. Beat in the rest of the milk and the melted butter or oil. Pour the batter into a jug ready for use.

Melt the vegetable fat in a small saucepan. Pour a little of the hot fat into the pancake pan. Quickly pour about 2 tablespoons of batter into the centre of the hot pan. Tip the pan so that the batter runs over the surface to make a thin pancake. Cook over moderate heat to brown the underside then turn. Repeat with each pancake.

Make a small pile of the filling in the middle of each pancake, top with a slice of tomato and fold the far edge of the pancake towards you to cover the filling, then fold the near edge over that; finish off the envelope shape by tucking the other two edges underneath. Heat the envelopes for about 3 minutes on each side.

Red clover salad and a collection of flowers to make wine. Photographed in the Yorkshire Dales, June 1.

Red Clover *Trifolium pratense* L. A perennial herb generally distributed throughout the British Isles, it occurs in grassy places, flowering from May to September.

Red clover is believed to have been first grown in this country as a cultivated crop in 1645. The American Indians ate it in several ways: the foliage was eaten fresh before flowering; the Digger tribe cooked it by placing moistened layers one upon another in a stone oven; and the Apache Indians boiled it with dandelions, grass and pigweed. The Pomo tribe held special clover feasts and dances in the early spring to celebrate the appearance of this food plant.

In Europe it is among the most generally cultivated fodder plants but is unknown as a human food. Its value as a food for cattle is reflected in the proverb 'to live in clover' and its ability to enrich the soil, and thus fertilize a following corn crop, gives rise to the saying that 'clover is the mother of corn'. To dream of clover foretells a happy marriage while a four-leaved clover gives the possessor the ability to see fairies. A two-leaved clover also has connections with marriage:

> *A clover, a clover of two, put it in your right shoe;*
> *The first young man you meet, in field, street or lane,*
> *You'll have him or one of his name.*

The normal three-leaved variety was often linked with the Holy Trinity.

Clover leaves can be cooked like spinach as a vegetable or they can be used in sandwiches, as can the flowers, and both flowers and leaves can be used as a flavouring or garnish.

Clover Salad

SERVES TWO

Clover leaves and blossoms
2 tablespoons olive oil
2 teaspoons finely chopped mint
75 g (3 oz) rice
2 tablespoons freshly squeezed orange juice

Cook the rice until tender in boiling, salted water, drain and mix with oil and orange juice while still hot. Wash the clover leaves, split into leaflets and trim stalks. Stir the clover leaves and chopped mint into the rice. Split the clover blossoms into florets and use as a garnish.

Red Clover Wine

2 litres (2 quarts) blossoms
4½ litres (1 gallon) water
3 lemons
2 oranges
1 kg (2.2 lb) sugar
1 packet of yeast

Pick the clover when it is well out but before the flowers start to go brown and put them in a plastic bucket. Bring the water to the boil and pour over the flowers, adding the juice of the oranges and lemons. Start the yeast to work in a glass with a little sugar and put near a radiator. By the time the water has cooled down to blood heat the yeast will have started and can be added to the bucket. Allow the must to ferment in the open bucket for 5 days. Strain into a jar, seal with an airlock and let it ferment until it has entirely stopped working. Rack it off into a clear jar and leave until it has completely settled out and then bottle. Alternatively, as you rack the wine off its sediment put it through a fine filter and bottle immediately. The wine will be white not red or pink as one might have hoped and if you ferment it in a rather warm room as I do, it may be a little too dry. If this is the case, a tiny amount of sugar syrup will sweeten it nicely. This is a light refreshing wine which can, and probably will, be drunk immediately.

Ash *Fraxinus excelsior* L. This is a common deciduous tree, generally distributed throughout the British Isles except in the Shetlands and the Scottish Highlands. It flowers in April and early May, then the keys develop in late May and may persist on the trees until November.

The ash tree is commonly found in folklore from all over Europe. The Yggdrasill-tree of Scandinavian mythology was an enormous ash whose roots spread in three directions: heaven, earth and hell. Under each root is a fountain of wonderful virtues while in the tree, which drops honey, are an eagle, a squirrel and four stags. There is a serpent, Nighhoggr, gnawing at the root, while the squirrel, Ratatoskr, runs up and down the trunk sowing strife between the eagle and the serpent. The legend also asserts that the gods made the first man, Askr, from ash wood. It was by using ash branches that witches were enabled to fly, although in Lincolnshire use of the female ash tree, called Sheder, would defeat a male witch, while the male tree, Heder, would defeat a female witch. Failure of the ash-seed crop was thought to foretell a royal death and a failure in 1648 was said to predict the execution of Charles I on January 1, 1649. A circle of ash twigs around the neck was said to cure an adder bite, while an ash leaf with an equal number of divisions on each side was thought to be lucky so that with 'The even-ash-leaf in my hand, the first I meet shall be my man'. As a wood for fuel, ash is said to be the best while still green but of little use when dry:

> Burn ash-wood green,
> 'Tis fire for a queen;
> Burn ash-wood sear,
> 'Twill make a man swear.

The only edible preparations from the ash are the keys, pickled, and the leaves, used as tea. Ash keys were held in high esteem by the ancient physicians. When pickled they were often used as a substitute for capers. Pick the very youngest keys for use.

Ash Key Pickle

This recipe comes from John Evelyn's *Acetaria, a Discourse of Sallets*, 1699:
'Gather them young, and boil them in three or four Waters to extract the Bitterness; and when they feel tender, prepare a Syrup of sharp White-Wine Vinegar, Sugar, and a little Water. Then boil them on a very quick Fire, and they will become of a green Colour, fit to be potted as soon as cold'.

This recipe is fine but be sure to gather the ash keys when they are very young for they quickly get too tough to be worth eating.

Sow Thistle *Sonchus oleraceus* L. The sow thistle is an annual or overwintering plant occurring throughout the British Isles. It is common everywhere except in the Scottish Highlands and occurs on cultivated soil, waysides and waste places. It flowers from June to September.

Sow thistles have been eaten as a vegetable since ancient times. The common English name was thought by William Coles, writing in the 17th century, to derive from 'a certain natural instinct' in sows to eat the plant when they had farrowed, as a herb to increase milk flow. Pliny tells us that Theseus dined on sow thistles, given to him by Hecate, before his victorious encounter with the Minotaur.

In the past, the leaves were boiled like spinach, cooked in soup and used as a pot-herb. The young leaves and young shoots were used raw on the Continent in salads. To cook the leaves, they can be steamed and seasoned with culinary herbs, oil and lemon juice.

Sow Thistle Salad

Use young leaves and shoots and some larger leaves with the soft spines trimmed away. I favour an ordinary French dressing so that the flavour of the thistle can be enjoyed and I find this makes a lovely, refreshing salad, rather crunchy in texture.

Ash key pickle. Photographed May 25.

Sow thistle can be found from April to June and also again in the autumn. Photographed May 12.

Fennel adds to the flavour of fish when you use it as a bed to grill on. Photographed in Cornwall, June 4.
I thought the tide was going out but it came in and my dinner floated away!

Fennel is common in waste places. Photographed June 3.

Rock samphire is an interesting vegetable with a strange, scented flavour. Photographed May 14.

Fennel *Foeniculum vulgare* Mill. Fennel is now a very common escape on roadsides, especially near the sea, and the leaves can be collected from May until November.

The Romans cultivated fennel for its aromatic seeds and the edible shoots, eaten as a vegetable. Roman bakers are said to have put the herb under their loaves to improve the flavour. The Anglo-Saxons also frequently used fennel in both cookery and medicine. Traditionally, fennel was grown to eat with fish, in particular with salt fish during Lent. Matthew Robinson, in *The New Family Herbal and Botanic Physician*, suggests 'One good old custom is not yet left off, viz. to boil Fennel with fish, for it consumes that phlegmatic humour, which fish copiously produces, though few know why they use it.'

In medieval times fennel was used as a preventative against witchcraft and other evil influences and was hung above doors at midsummer. It was believed to restore lost vision and to give courage and was included in victory wreaths, as told by Longfellow in 'The Goblet of Life':

More recently it has been eaten with salmon, to correct the fish's oily indigestibility, and in a sauce with boiled mackerel. Other uses include the leaves as garnishes and in salads and sauces; the very young stems in salads and soups; and the seeds in confectionery and as a flavouring for drinks.

> *It gave new strength and fearless mood,*
> *And gladiators fierce and rude*
> *Mingled it in their daily food;*
> *And he who battled and subdued,*
> *The wreath of Fennel wore.*

Snakes are said to eat fennel before sloughing their skins to renew their youth but for those who sought to cultivate it, 'Sow fennel, sow trouble'.

Charcoal Grilled Fish on Fennel

Collect stems and leaves of well-grown fennel and hang them upside down in the sun to dry. They can be then be kept for months or used once they are dry enough to burn.

Take any fish suitable for grilling: trout, mackerel, mullet – the more oily fish are best. Clean out the fish (leaving on the head) and stuff with fresh fennel leaves, butter and slices of lemon. Put a good bed of dried fennel sticks over your grill and place the fish on top. The sticks will soon catch alight but do not lose faith because it is this burning of the fennel that gives the fish its special flavour. Let the fish cook on both sides until it begins to break up slightly when prodded. Serve with a fennel sauce to really emphasize the flavour.

Fennel Sauce

35 g (1½ oz) butter
25 g (1 oz) plain flour

Salt and pepper
1 heaped tablespoon chopped fennel
4½ dl (¾ pint) milk

Melt 25 g (1 oz) butter and cook the fennel in it for 30 seconds. Blend in the flour and cook for 1 minute, stirring well. Work in the milk and simmer until the sauce is creamy and smooth. Season to taste with salt and pepper and stir in the remaining butter. Serve with grilled mackerel and other fish.

This recipe comes from Mary Norwak and I have found it to be an exciting accompaniment, especially to dull white fish.

Fennel Bulb or Root

You can buy fennel bulbs in the shops which may be chopped up and used in salads. This is not from the same plant that you find growing in the wild, for those roots are not edible as they are sometimes said to be. They are, in fact, tough and unpleasant without the sweet aniseed taste of the rest of the plant.

Rock Samphire *Crithmum maritimum* L. This perennial herb occurs on the coast from Ayr to Cornwall and eastwards to Kent and Suffolk and also on the coasts of Ireland and the isles of Lewis and Islay. It is found hanging in tassels on cliffs and rocks or, more rarely, on shingle or sand by the sea. It flowers from June to September but the leaves are at their best and freshest between spring and early summer, before the flowers appear.

Rock samphire was at one time cultivated in English gardens for its seed pods and used to be cried in London streets as 'Crest Marine'. The stems, leaves and seed pods may be picked if sprinkled with salt, boiled and covered with vinegar and spices. The popularity of the pickle is due to the warm, aromatic flavour of the plant. Robinson considers 'it makes a fine pickle, which was formerly highly esteemed. The sale of it has been almost stopped by adulteration,' and Hill agrees: 'The leaves are used fresh; but those which grow immediately from the Root, where there is no stalk are best; They are pickled, and brought to our Tables; but they are often adulterated, and other Things pickled in their Place.'

Rock samphire may be used in salads or cooked as a vegetable. Before cooking remove any leaves that have begun to turn slimy and any hard parts of the stalk. The name samphire comes from 'herbe de St Pierre', the herb of the fishermen's saint.

Rock Samphire Boiled

Wash the samphire well and remove any tough stalks or leaves that have begun to turn slimy. Leave the white roots intact. Boil in water for 10-15 minutes and serve with plenty of melted butter. To eat, hold the plant by the root, dip it in butter and then suck the fleshy part away from the fibrous veins.

Brooklime can be used in salads in place of watercress. Photographed May 10.

Coltsfoot leaves make a tasty vegetable. Photographed June 10.

Brooklime *Veronica beccabunga* L. Brooklime is a native perennial common throughout the British Isles and found growing in streams, ponds, marshes and wet places in meadows. It flowers from May to September.

Brooklime can be used in salads but it is more bitter than watercress. John Hill in *The British Herbal*, 1756, suggests: 'A large quantity of this herb put into beer, while brewing, gives it the virtues of an anti-scorbutick and sweetner of the blood in a very happy manner.'

Coltsfoot Cream

Chop and sauté a handful or two of small coltsfoot leaves. Add water to cover and cook until soft. Add a tablespoon of toasted sesame seeds to the strained leaves and beat into an even cream.

Reproduced from *The Urban Dweller's Country Almanac* by Bernard Scholfield, 1978, with the permission of the publishers, Cassell & Co. Ltd.

This is a very tasty dish; the combination of the sesame seeds and the coltsfoot leaves is well worth trying. I found it is just as good if you serve it without going to the lengths of beating it to a cream. The main entry for coltsfoot is on page 26.

Plantain *Plantago major* L. This is listed as a salad herb or a vegetable in many books. I have tried it a few times both cooked and raw but I find it horrible to eat because it is tough and bitter.

Watercress *Rorippa nasturtium-aquaticum* (L.) Hayeck. Watercress is a lowland plant, common throughout Britain except in the Scottish Highlands and central Wales. It is found in streams ditches and flushes with moving water. It can be gathered at almost any time, except when there is a frost, and it flowers from May to October.

There is documentary evidence that watercress was used as a medicinal plant from the first century AD (Dioscorides's *Materia Medica* of about AD 77) to the 19th century. It was not cultivated until the 19th century but it seems probable that plants must often have been spread by man.

Large-scale cultivation in England was started in Gravesend in 1808 to supply the Covent Garden Market in London and it was sold in large quantities in other cities up until a century ago. A staple food in these islands until modern times, it was a valuable source of vitamin C. It was traditionally used as a garnish for parsnips and was cooked with or in place of nettles in gruels and soups. With boiled bacon watercress was a traditional Irish dish before the advent of cabbage. The Latin name *nasturtium* is derived from *nasus tortus*, a convulsed nose, on account of its pungency.

Pick the more mature shoots; on some plants the leaves have a bronze tint, on others they are dark green. Do not pull the plant up by the roots but cut the tops off the shoots. Wash thoroughly and use promptly. Do not refrigerate as this destroys the texture.

When collecting wild watercress the fear is of liver fluke. Stan Williams who owns a watercress farm told me that the danger spreads from cattle but more especially from sheep. If the cress is growing by a stream where there are no sheep or cattle in any stretch above where you are it will be fine to eat fresh; but, if there are cattle present the cress should be very thoroughly washed before eating raw. However, if the watercress is cooked any danger will be removed so I tend to think of wild watercress soup as the ideal way of eating it.

Watercress Soup

SERVES FOUR
2 bunches watercress
2 large potatoes
Generous knob of butter
Dash of vegetable oil (to stop butter burning)
1 chicken stock cube
Salt and freshly ground black pepper
Single cream

Put the butter in a large saucepan with dash of oil and melt over a low flame. Place a mandolin over the saucepan and slice the potatoes (or cube them). Cook very gently until the potatoes are soft. Dissolve the stock cube in the boiling water and add to the saucepan, simmering for 15 minutes. Then add the watercress (coarsely chopped) and simmer for a further 7 minutes (retain some watercress leaves for the garnish). Liquidize, stir in some single cream and chill in the fridge. Decorated with fresh watercress leaves, it makes a delightful summer soup.

This recipe, which comes from Pammy Williams, is equally delicious served either cold in the summer or hot in the winter.

Watercress soup is one of the staples of a wild food kitchen. Photographed in Ireland, May 13.

Candied angelica showing the giant plants behind. Photographed on an island in the Thames, May 20.

Angelica *Angelica archangelica* L. This is the French angelica which is cultivated in traditional kitchen gardens. It can sometimes be found growing in the wild as an escape, usually on river banks or islands, and when you come across it it may well be abundant. It flowers from the middle of June but the stems which you cut to make candied angelica should be collected at the end of April or during May. The leaves can also be used sparingly in salads and with boiled fruit.

The native British angelica *Angelica sylvestris* L. is not good to eat being both tough and bitter.

To Candy Angelica

While the stalks are tender cut them into lengths of 8-10 cm (3-4 in). Place in a pan, cover with a tight-fitting lid and boil with very little water. Peel them, boil again until green and then dry with a cloth. Put 450 g (1 lb) of sugar to 450 g (1 lb) of the stalks in an earthenware pan. Let it stand covered for two days, then boil the angelica and sugar till clear and green and put into a colander to drain. Strew as much pounded castor sugar over as will adhere to it and let it dry, but not become hard, in a slack oven. This is time-consuming!

Made fresh like this candied angelica is infinitely superior to the shop-bought variety and in fact, when I made it, none was kept for cake making – it was all nibbled up in an hour or two!

Sea Purslane *Halimione portulacoides* (L.) Aell. Sea purslane can be found in abundance on salt marshes below the high tide mark and especially fringing channels and pools in salt marshes. It flowers from July to September.

When collecting sea purslane good wellington boots are an essential piece of equipment as it often grows in clumps surrounded by deep, treacherous mud. It is a bit fiddly to wash and clean away the old weed from the leaves but their interesting flavour as a vegetable makes it well worthwhile. Nice leaves can be found at almost any time during the year.

Sea Purslane Vegetable

SERVES TWO
350 g (12 oz) purslane leaves
25 g (1 oz) butter

Sea purslane as a vegetable. Photographed on the salt marsh at St John's, Cornwall, June 4.

2 teaspoons chopped parsley
Juice of ½ lemon
Salt and pepper

Cook the purslane leaves with a lid on the pan, in just enough boiling water to cover them. When tender, drain well. Add butter, parsley, lemon juice and seasoning and shake over heat for a few minutes. Serve immediately.

To Pickle Purslain

'Take Purslain, Stalks and all, boil them in fair Water, and lay them to dry upon a Linen Cloth. When they are thorough dry put them into Gally-pots and cover them with White-wine Vingar in which Salt has been dissolved.' Pickled purslane is still made and sold in jars in France.

This old recipe is from Carter, 1736.

A bowl of the lovely mallow melokhia soup. Photographed June 5.

Common Mallow *Malva sylvestris* L. A common perennial throughout England, less frequent in Wales and Ireland, and only local in Scotland, mallow does not occur in the Outer Hebrides, Orkney and Shetland. It is found on roadsides and waste places, flowering from June to October.

The common name is derived from the Old English 'malwe', meaning soft, referring to the soft, downy leaves. The Romans are said to have eaten mallow leaves as a vegetable, as did the ancient Egyptians and Chinese. The seeds of the mallow, known as 'cheeses' because of their shape, were also eaten by country people and the plant has been used to supply a purgative drug.

The leaves are best picked in the summer when they are pale and stretch like gelatine. They should always be washed well. Discard any that have developed a brownish rust or are embedded with black insect eggs.

Our native mallow is very similar in texture and flavour to melokhia *Carchorus olitorius* L. which is much grown in Arab countries, particularly Egypt, where it is used to make melokhia soup, one of the staple foods.

Mallow Melokhia Soup

SERVES FOUR
2 litres (3 pints) chicken stock
750 g (nearly 2 lb) mallow leaves
3 tablespoons olive oil
4 cloves garlic
1 tablespoon ground coriander
A good pinch of cayenne pepper
Salt

Pick only young, fresh mallow leaves, the older leaves are too fibrous and should be discarded. Wash and chop the leaves as finely as you can. I use a Chinese chopping axe and find that this way I can make a fine pulp. The chicken stock is best if it's home-made, especially if you use a chicken which still has bits of stuffing in it. Leeks or root vegetables also make a stock richer so if you don't have a chicken carcass to make the stock from use root vegetables and a chicken stock cube. Strain off the stock, bring it to the boil, add the chopped mallow leaves and boil for 10 minutes. In a small pan, fry the crushed garlic and salt. As it starts to brown add the coriander and cayenne pepper, mix it into a paste over the heat, then add to the main soup, stirring it well in. Cook for 3 minutes and serve.

Mallow melokhia can be served in several ways: either as a soup with coarse brown bread; or with a bowl of rice; or with pieces of meat or meatballs added. All are tasty.

I have adapted this recipe from the melokhia recipe in Claudia Roden's excellent book *A Book of Middle Eastern Food,* 1968.

Salad Burnet *Poterium sanguisorba* L. A perennial herb, widespread and common, it occurs in calcareous grassland and flowers from May to August.

Salad burnet was taken by the Pilgrim Fathers to the New World. Matthew Robinson in *The New Family Herbal* says about the herb: 'The continual use of it preserves the body in health and the mind in vigour . . . Two or three of the stalks, with leaves put into a cup of wine, especially claret, are known to quicken the spirits and drive away melancholy.'

The leaves can be added to salads but use very sparingly, as they have a strong, bitter flavour.

Salad Burnet Drink

Bruise half a dozen sprays of salad burnet and place in a large jug. Add a bottle of hock and 3 wineglassfuls of sherry plus a sliced lemon. Leave to stand for 2 hours, sweetening to taste, then add a bottle of soda water and serve with crushed ice.

Red Valerian *Centranthus ruber* (L.) DC. This has white and pink forms and is quite common, growing wild near the sea usually among rocks and on cliffs. The young leaves are edible when boiled but I found them too bitter to be worthwhile.

Common mallow is found in profusion on roadsides and waste ground.
Photographed June 6.

Red valerian is quite common around the coast, and as a garden flower.
Photographed June 5.

Salad burnet drink. Photographed in the Cheddar Gorge, June 20.

Oar weed cut into small squares and deep fried for tasty chips. Photographed March 31.

Sea lettuce served with cream. Photographed May 27.

Sweet Oar Weed *Laminaria saccharina* L. Very common around our coasts, growing at the low tide mark and below it, it has fronds up to 3 m (10 ft). It can be found at all times of year but is especially succulent in the spring.

Oar Weed Chips

Collect a nice, fresh frond of oar weed and leave it hung up in the kitchen to dry, then cut it into 2 cm (¾ in) squares and fry it in a light oil like sesame seed oil. The squares will expand very quickly and start to brown. Remove them after a few seconds and drain on kitchen paper. These salty chips are ideal as an appetizer with drinks.

Sea Lettuce *Ulva lactuca* L. The fronds, which are thin, translucent green, leaf-shaped or sometimes lobed, can be up to 50 cm (1 ft 6 in) long. They are common all round our coasts on rocks, usually near the high tide area.

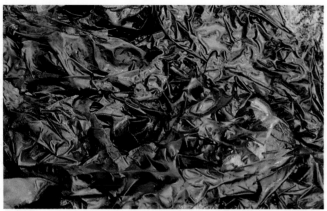

Sea lettuce growing near the high tide mark. Photographed June 3.

Sea Lettuce Salad

SERVES TWO
6 dl (1 pint) sea lettuce
3 spring onions
1½ dl (¼ pint) cream
Juice of ½ lemon
½ tablespoon cider vinegar
1 tablespoon olive oil
Cayenne pepper

Wash the sea lettuce well and chop into bite-sized pieces. Toss in butter for 3 minutes over a low heat, allow to cool, then place a small portion in each individual bowl. Make a dressing by lightly shaking together the cream, lemon juice, cider vinegar and olive oil. Pour over the sea lettuce, decorating with pieces of spring onion and a pinch of cayenne pepper.

Sea Lettuce Vinaigrette

25 g (1 oz) sea lettuce
Japanese rice vinegar
1 tablespoon sukiyaki sauce

Place the sea lettuce in a small bowl and cover with rice vinegar (cider vinegar and 1 tablespoon of sugar may be used as a substitute). Put the sukiyaki sauce in a separate bowl. Take pieces of sea lettuce and dip into sukiyaki sauce. Serve as an appetizer leaving the sea lettuce in the vinegar. This recipe can be made with dulse or dulse and sea lettuce mixed. The Japanese also add spinach, shredded Chinese radish, raw mackeral and cucumber and garnish with a carrot flower.

Enteromorpha is an excellent crisp dish when stir fried. Photographed April 22.

Enteromorpha intestinalis (L.) Link. Very common around our coasts just below the high tide level in pools, on rocks and in estuaries, it occurs from spring onwards. Pick fresh green fronds, which can be as long as 1 m (3 ft).

Stir Fried Enteromorpha

Wash and clean the enteromorpha thoroughly and then heat a light oil, like sunflower seed oil, in a wok or ordinary saucepan. Take the enteromorpha in small handfuls, quickly fry until crisp and serve immediately.

This is a delicious dish very similar to the crispy, fried seaweed served in some Chinese restaurants. It is well worth trying, especially as in many areas it is so common. It can also be added to salads.

Enteromorpha growing near the high tide mark. Photographed May 28.

Oak leaf wine fermenting near East Looe. Photographed June 3.

Oak *Quercus robur* L. Common all over the British Isles, the leaves start to come at the end of May. Acorns normally ripen in October and can be roasted and used as a coffee substitute but I hesitate, as I found this a most unpalatable drink.

Oak Leaf Wine

4½ litres (1 gallon) oak leaves
4½ litres (1 gallon) water
1 kg (2.2 lb) sugar
3 oranges
Yeast
Pectinol

Pick the oak leaves when they are very young and fresh; normally this will be the last week of May or the beginning of June. Boil the water and pour it onto the oak leaves, leaving over night. Strain out the leaves and boil the liquid for 20 minutes, then add the sugar and orange juice and the grated rind. When the liquid has cooled to blood heat add the yeast, leave to ferment in an open bucket for five days and transfer to a fermentation jar. Fit an airlock and leave to ferment until it stops working and the sediment settles. At this point rack off into a clean jar, add Pectinol to remove the haze, leave for 24 hours and then filter the wine off into sterilized bottles and cork down with corks that have been boiled for 10 minutes.

This recipe has come down to me from Violet Ricketts, although I have altered it a little to make a drier wine. It is a most successful recipe and was quite delicious immediately it was bottled. In fact, although most books say that all wines should be kept for six months before drinking, I find that these light white wines are generally at their best when very young.

Beech leaf noyau is a must for anyone keen on home-made wines. Photographed May 25.

Walnut Leaf Wine

This is made in exactly the same way as the oak leaf wine but it seems that less leaves are needed, say only 3 litres. Using the recipe above, I ended up with a lovely, dry white wine.

Beech *Fagus sylvatica* L. Very common especially on chalk hills, the young leaves are at their best in the last week of April or during May when they develop with the flowers.

Beech Leaf Noyau

1 bottle gin
225 g (8 oz) white sugar
1 glass of brandy

Collect young, fresh beech leaves and strip them from the twigs. Half fill an empty bottle or jar with the leaves and then pour on the bottle of gin. Seal up the container and keep leaves in it for 3 weeks, before straining them off. Boil the sugar in 3 dl (½ pint) of water and add this to the gin with a good sized glass of brandy. You should end up with two almost-full bottles of noyau for the price of one bottle of gin. Believe me it's worth every penny. It is a liquor that every one of my fussy friends has gone mad for.

This recipe is based on Richard Mabey's recipe in *Food for Free*, 1972.

Elderflower champagne and water ice. Photographed June 15.

Elder *Sambucus nigra* L. A deciduous shrub or small tree common throughout the British Isles excepting northern Scotland, it occurs in woods, scrub, roadsides and waste places. The elder flowers in June and July and bears fruit in August and September.

The flower clusters should be cut whole from the tree with about 5 cm (1 in) of stem attached. Check the clusters for insects and discard any that are badly infested. However, do not wash the flowers as this will remove much of the fragrance. Pick the flowers in the last weeks of June or the first days of July. Recipes for the berries are on pages 118-19.

The word 'elder' is derived from the Anglo-Saxon *aeld*, meaning fire, because the hollow branches were used to blow up the flames of fires. The generic name *Sambucus* is used by Pliny and is derived from the Greek *sambuca* referring to the Roman musical instrument. The elder has often been thought of as the witches' tree

and many charms are connected with it. It is a favourite form for a witch to assume and an elder which was a transformed witch would bleed if it was cut. However, the power of the elder can also be used against witches and any baptized person whose eyes are touched with the green juice of the inner bark of the elder can see what witches are up to in any part of the world.

In the Isle of Man it was said that an elder tree was to be found growing by every old cottage and that these were planted to protect the inhabitants against witchcraft. On May-eve the leaves would be picked and fixed to doors and windows for extra protection. In Shropshire, it was believed that a death in the family would follow the use of elder in the fireplace and that furniture made of elderwood would warp, creak or break. On the Scottish border elder is said to grow only where blood has been shed but it could be planted near a grave to protect the body after death; if planted on the grave and seen to blossom it indicated the happiness of the soul beneath.

Elderwood will protect the bearer against rheumatism or saddle-soreness and the leaves, if bruised, will keep flies away. Tradition has it that Judas hanged himself on an an elder. The young stems of the elder contain a soft pith which can be easily pushed out to give a hollow tube. The Italian peasants used these stems to make a simple pipe or *sampogna*, while country lads in Britain used the stems for whistles or simple pop-guns. Shakespeare, in *Henry V*, mentions a 'perilous shot out of an elder-gun'.

Elder flowers have been much used in country districts in the past. Bunches were hung indoors to keep away flies and the blossoms were beaten into the batter of flannel cakes and muffins to give a more delicate texture. John Evelyn, 1664, recommends the blossom infused in vinegar as a salad ingredient and in their unripened state the blossoms could be pickled as a substitute for capers. In Victorian times, every household kept a bottle of elderflower water for removing freckles and sunburn.

Elderflower Champagne

4 elderflower heads in full bloom
4½ litres (1 gallon) cold water
1 lemon
650 g (1½ lb) loaf sugar
2 tablespoons white vinegar

Dissolve the sugar in a little warm water and allow to cool. Squeeze the juice from the lemon, cut the rind in four, put the pieces with the elderflowers in a large jug or basin, add the wine vinegar and pour on the rest of the cold water. Leave to steep for 4 days. Strain off and bottle in screw-topped bottles. It should be ready to drink in 6 to 10 days but test after 6 days anyway to see that it does not get too fizzy. If it fails to work leave it for another week; sometimes the natural yeast of the flowers is very slow to get going and occasionally you will get a batch that fails altogether. Some people say you should pick the flowers on a sunny day but I have picked them in the rain and had success with them.

I advise everyone to make this fragrant champagne. It is really a most refreshing summer drink served chilled or with ice and lemon. This recipe was given to me by Irene Palmer.

Elderflower Wine or Frontiniac

This recipe came to me from Ted Rix who got it from his aunt, Melba Stunt, and the actual recipe had the date 1736 pencilled on it. I have adjusted the quantities a little in testing it.

6 dl (1 pint) elderflowers, trimmed from the bunch and pressed well down
1 kg (2.2 lb) sugar
450 g (1 lb) raisins
Juice of 2 lemons
4½ litres (1 gallon) water
1 well-beaten egg white

Boil the water, sugar, raisins and white of egg together for 1 hour. Start the yeast. Allow the liquid to cool, then stir in elderflowers, lemon juice and yeast. Leave to ferment in a bucket for 3 days and then put it in a fermenting jar to work itself out. When it is completely clear siphon it off into sterilized bottles, cork with sterilized corks and then keep for at least 3 months before drinking. I found that I got a haze in mine so I used Pectinol to clear it and then filtered it out after 24 hours. This wine is an exception amongst the white wines I have made in that it definitely improves with keeping.

Elderflower Fritters

SERVES FOUR
100 g (4 oz) flour
1 egg
1½ dl (¼ pint) tepid water
Pinch of salt
Unwashed flowerheads of elder

Melilot flowering. Photographed June 9.

Make a batter using all the ingredients except the elderflowers. Hold the flowerheads by their stalks and dip into the batter until thoroughly coated. Deep fry the flowerheads in very hot fat or oil until golden brown. Drain on kitchen paper and trim excess stalk. Serve hot, sprinkled with sugar.

To Pickle Elder-buds

'Boil Water and Salt together, put in the Buds and let them boil a while; but not till they are tender, then strain them, and set them by to cool. In the meantime boil White-wine Vinegar with two Blades of Mace, and a little whole Pepper. Put the Buds into the Pickle and let them stand nine Days, then scald them in a Brass Kettle six several times, till they are as green as Grass; but take care they do not grow soft. Then put them into Pots, and tye them down with Leather.'
The Compleat City and Country Cook by Charles Carter, 1736.

Elderflower Lemonade

Cover 2 litres (4 pints) of fresh elderflowers with 2 litres (4 pints) of water. Add 1 sliced lemon, a tablespoon of malt or cider vinegar and 300 g (10 oz) sugar. Stir well and leave for 24 hours. Strain and simmer mixture for 15 minutes then leave and bottle when cool. Chill before serving.

Reproduced from *The Urban Dweller's Country Almanac* by Bernard Schofield, 1978, by permission of the publishers, Cassell & Co. Ltd.

Elderflower Water Ice

SERVES FOUR
7½ dl (1¼ pints) water
100 g (4 oz) sugar
175 ml (6 fl oz) lemon juice
2 tablespoons grated lemon rind
25 g (1 oz) dried elderflowers

In a heavy pan bring water and sugar to boil over a moderate heat, stirring constantly, and wash down any sugar crystals clinging to the sides of the pan with a brush dipped in cold water, until sugar has dissolved. Boil the syrup for 5 minutes then stir in the lemon juice and rind. Put the elderflowers in a double thickness of cheesecloth and tie ends with string. Add to the mixture and heat for 5 minutes. Remove pan from heat and cool. Remove elderflowers and squeeze out excess liquid. Pour mixture into freezing containers and freeze, stirring every hour for 4 hours, or until ice is well blended and firm.

Pamela Harlech's recipe for Elderflower Water Ice is reprinted from Vogue, 1975, by kind permission of Condé Nast Publications.

Melilot *Melilotus officinalis* (L.) Pall. A biennial herb, naturalized in south England and infrequent elsewhere, it is found in fields and on roadsides and waste places and it flowers from July to September. The leaves, if gathered before the flowers appear, are said to be a useful vegetable but I find them bitter in the extreme.

Broom bud salad is a stunning colour combination. Photographed May 10.

Broom wine has an extraordinary, dry flavour. Photographed June 10.

Broom *Sarothamnus scoparius* (L.) Wimmer ex Koch. Broom is generally distributed throughout the British Isles except for Orkney and Shetland. It occurs on heaths, waste ground and in woods, usually on sandy soils, and flowers from March to June. Pick the young flower buds in late April, May or June.

The green twigs of the broom have long been used for sweeping and it is from this that the household 'broom' gets its name. It is considered unlucky to take the broom into the house during May, particularly to use it for sweeping, because

If you sweep the house with broom in May,
You'll sweep the head of that house away.

The profusion of flowers borne by the broom has made it a symbol of good luck and plenty and for this reason a bundle of green broom tied with ribbons was often taken to country weddings. However, the flowers themselves contain very little nectar and are rather bitter, giving rise to the saying 'He bestows his gifts as the broom does honey'. In contrast to this, however, an old proverb states that 'Under the furze is hunger and cold; under the broom is silver and gold'.

Henry II of England threaded the yellow flowers of the broom into his helmet when going into battle so that his men could easily recognize him. The plant was adopted into Henry's heraldic crest and its medieval name, *planta genista,* gave the name 'Plantagenets' to his line. An even older tradition suggests that when Mary and Joseph were fleeing into Egypt, Mary cursed the broom because the crackling of its ripe pods as they passed risked drawing the attention of Herod's soldiers.

The bark of the broom yields an excellent fibre, separated by macerating the twigs in water, like flax, and this has been used from ancient times. Fibrous matter in the shoots has also been used to make paper and cloth. Drugs obtained from the broom are used to treat liver and kidney infections and heart disease, while Henry VII drank broom tea for indigestion. Before the introduction of hops, the tender green tops of the broom were often used to give a bitter flavour to beer and to render it more intoxicating, while the roasted seeds have been used on the Continent as a coffee substitute. Until recently broom buds were regarded as a delicacy, traditionally served as an appetizer, and they are known to have been included in the Coronation feast of James II, while in English country districts they were a favourite substitute for pickled capers.

It is essential to distinguish carefully between Spanish broom *Spartium junceum* and true broom, since a number of cases of poisoning have occurred from the substitution of the dried flowers of *Spartium* for those of broom. Spanish broom is most easily distinguished by the leaves which are narrow, rather like a pine needle; true broom, however, has small leaves that are more oval in shape and grouped in bunches of three. Broom flowers from the end of April to June whereas Spanish broom flowers later, normally from the end of June to August.

Broom Bud Salad

SERVES TWO
1 cupful broom buds
2 large tomatoes
6 button mushrooms
Cress, French dressing

Carefully pick the flowerbuds so that they are clean and ready to use in the salad. Cut the tomatoes and mushrooms into fine slices. As the broom buds are so colourful I think it is worthwhile making a really decorative arrangement of the ingredients or alternatively, they can be mixed together and tossed with dressing as for a normal salad. The broom flowers have an odd, dry, nutty flavour which is a distinctive addition to a salad.

Broom Flower Wine

2 litres (4 pints) broom flowers
1 kg (2.2 lb) sugar
2 oranges, 2 lemons
4½ litres (1 gallon) water
Yeast

Pick broom flowers that have opened and place them in a bucket with the juice of the oranges and lemons. Boil the water with the sugar and the zest of the oranges and lemons, pour onto the broom

Spruce beer is well worth making. A favourite drink of the Russians. Photographed (whilst being attacked by 8 million gnats) June 6.

flowers and stir well. Put on the yeast to start. When the liquid has cooled to blood heat, add the yeast and leave it to ferment for 4 days in a warm place. Then, strain off the solids and transfer to a fermenting jar with an airlock. When the wine has completely stopped working filter it off and bottle in sterilized bottles and cork with sterilized corks.

The broom gives this wine a very strange, dry flavour in the mouth which I like but Jacqui, my assistant, finds quite unpalatable. It may be necessary to sweeten the wine a little to combat this.

Pickle Broom-buds

'Take the Buds before they grown yellow on the top, make a Brine for them of Vinegar and Salt, shaking them together while the Salt is melted; then put in the Buds; stir them once a day, 'till they suck in the Pickle, and keep them close cover'd.'

This is an old recipe from John Carter's *The Compleat City and Country Cook*, 1736.

Spruce Norway spruce *Picea abies* or Sitka spruce *P. sitchensis*. These are the two most common species found in Britain and either may be used for this recipe. Danzig, in Prussia, was and is famous for spruce beer; in Britain the beverage was considered very poor stuff. This gave rise to the Cockney rhyming slang 'bottle of spruce' i.e. 'deuce' (meaning tuppence), an expression used to refer to worthless objects or suggestions. A consignment of 'essence of spruce, and other extra stores adapted to cold climates and a long voyage' was taken by Captain Davy on his voyage of discovery for the North-west Passage in 1819.

Spruce Beer

40 young spruce twigs
350 g (12 oz) sugar
100 g (4 oz) treacle
4½ litres (1 gallon) water
Yeast

Gather the fresh new twigs from any species of spruce in May or June and boil them in the water for 30 minutes. Start the yeast. Strain off the liquid and mix in the sugar and treacle while it is still hot. Either dark or light treacle can be used. When cool, add the yeast, allow to ferment in a bucket for 6 days, then scoop off the scum and siphon into bottles. Check daily to see the beer does not get too fizzy. The beer can be drunk after about a week in the bottles. In Germany it is made with dark treacle and no sugar to give a strong-flavoured black beer. You can also add ginger and spices. I always make it with light treacle as it seems to me black treacle gives too dominating a flavour, but including a little horseradish, as the Russians do, is an excellent addition.

Horseradish sauce served with baron of beef. Photographed at Grange Gill Force, June 23.

Horseradish *Armoracia rusticana* Gaertn., Mey & Scherb. The horseradish is a perennial herb, naturalized throughout Great Britain northwards to Moray, although it is infrequent in the south-west. It occurs in fields, roadsides and waste places and flowers from May to September.

Cultivation of horseradish in its native area (eastern Europe and Turkey) has been practised for at least 2000 years and the plant was referred to by Dioscorides. The Germans and Slavs were probably the first people in Europe to use it, grated in sauces and pickles, and its use as a condiment reached England between 1597 and 1640. Before this time, both the root and leaves were used universally as a medicine and it was one of the bitter herbs eaten by the Jews during Passover. John Pechey, writing in the 17th century, says of it, 'It provokes the Appetite, but it hurts the Head.' The prefix 'horse' means coarse as in horse-mint and horse-chestnut.

The plant gets easier to find as the year progresses because the large, long and beautifully shiny leaves become a dominant feature of road banks.

A spade is essential when gathering horseradish as, being perennial, the plant carries an extensive and complex root system. Pare away the brown layer using a sharp knife and grate the root for use. This is best done out of doors.

Home-made Horseradish Sauce

50 g (2 oz) fresh horseradish
1½ dl (¼ pint) double cream
1 teaspoon sugar
½ teaspoon mustard powder
½ teaspoon salt
½ teaspoon white pepper
2 teaspoons white wine vinegar

Leave the root of the horseradish soaking in cold water for 1 hour, then wash well and scrape clean. Grate the horseradish or cut it into very thin shreds with a sharp knife. Whip the cream to soft peaks and fold in the horseradish, sugar, mustard, salt, pepper and vinegar. Serve cold with beef.

This recipe comes from Mary Norwak and the fresh sauce made like this is streets ahead of the shop-bought variety. It can also be made using the horseradish pickle in place of fresh horseradish. Rinse it thoroughly before use and then squeeze out the excess liquid, otherwise fold it into the cream in the same way.

Horseradish leaves are easy to spot from June onwards. Photographed June 25.

Wild clary, too rare to use in modern times. Photographed June 25.

Horseradish Pickle

Grated horseradish
White vinegar, cooking salt

Use the roots when they have been freshly dug. Wash very well in hot water and scrape off the skin. Grate the roots or mince finely and pack firmly but not too tightly into small jars. Use 1 teaspoon of salt to each 3 dl (½ pint) of vinegar, mix well and cover the horseradish. Seal tightly with vinegar-proof lids. This grated horseradish may be drained and made into horseradish sauce or added to other dishes.

Another recipe from Mary Norwak.

Horseradish makes the eyes run – it is almost worse than onions – so be prepared for tears when preparing roots.

Horseradish and Potato Salad

SERVES TWO
450 g (1 lb) potatoes
2 tablespoons grated horseradish
Salt
Parsley, finely chopped
Yoghurt

Boil the potatoes until tender, leave to cool and then chop. Mix the horseradish, finely chopped parsley and salt and stir into the yoghurt. Add the potato.

Wild Clary *Salvia horminoides* Pourr. This perennial herb is a rare plant of southern England and because of this I feel that it should not really be eaten. However, as it is so well known historically I have included some old recipes. It occurs locally in dry pastures and roadsides, and flowers from May to August.

Meadow Clary *Salvia pratensis* L. The larger flowered clary is very rare in Britain but may be found on roadsides in Europe. Perhaps it was this plant that the medieval herbalists grew and used so constantly.

The name is a corruption of the Latin *clarus*, meaning 'clear', and has been further corrupted, in some country districts, into 'Clear Eye', reputedly from the fact that the seeds have been employed for clearing the sight. Matthew Robinson, in *The New Family Herbal*, gives directions as follows: 'It is a capital remedy for dimness of sight. The plan is to put the seed into the eyes. They immediately collect a coat of mucilage about them and this catches hold of any little thing it meets with in the eye – the seeds drop out of themselves, and cause little pain.'

The herb was first used in Germany by wine merchants who infused it with elderflowers and used the resultant liquid to adulterate Rhenish wine, thereby converting it into Muscatel. The German name for the herb is 'Muskateller Salbei' or muscatel sage. In some parts of this country, a wine has been made from the herb in flower, boiled with sugar, which has a flavour not unlike Frontiniac. Before hops were introduced clary was used to flavour ale: 'Some brewers of ale do put it in their drink to make it more heady, fit to please drunkards.' Apparently it endowed the beer with considerable bitterness and intoxicating properties, which produced an effect of insane exhilaration succeeded by severe headache!

Clary Wine

'Take twelve pounds of Malage Raisins, after they have been pick'd small and chop'd, put them into a Vessel, and a quart of Water to each pound. Let them stand to steep for ten or twelve Days, being kept close cover'd all the while stirring them twice every Day: afterwards strain it off, and put it up in a Cask, adding a quarter of a Peck of the Tops of Clary, when it is in Blossom; then stop it up close for six Weeks, and afterwards you may bottle it off, and it will be fit to drink in two or three Months. It will have a great Settlement, therefore it should be tapp'd pretty high, or drawn off by Plugs.'

From Carter's *Herbal*, 1736.

Meadow clary, the larger flowered species, more commonly grown in gardens.
Photographed August 1.

Burdock boiled dry is a really good Japanese-style vegetable. Photographed June 24.

Burdock and dandelion beer. This is a dark version made mainly with molasses. Photographed June 29.

Roasted Burdock

Roll whole, cleaned burdock root in fresh, young burdock leaves, then wrap in silver foil. Roast in hot ashes for about 45-60 minutes. Serve with soy sauce. In Japan, people living in the mountains eat the roots prepared like this in autumn and winter.

Both the above recipes have been adapted from *The Chico-san Cookbook* by Cornellia Aihara.

Burdock Beer

3 good sized burdock roots.
450 g (1 lb) sugar
2 heaped tablespoons molasses or black treacle
1 lemon
Yeast
4½ litres (1 gallon) water

Burdock roots should be collected just as the plants begin to make their leaves. Scrub the roots absolutely clean and then chop them up into small pieces. Boil them for 20 minutes in half the water. Put the yeast to start. Add the sugar and molasses to the hot water to dissolve, then add the juice of the lemon, strain out the solids and make the liquid up to the full amount. When cool, add the yeast. Leave to ferment in the bucket for four days and then bottle it off in screw-topped bottles. Test daily to see it does not get too fizzy. It can be drunk after one week. If you prefer a flavour more like Guinness you can increase the amount of molasses and decrease the amount of sugar to taste.

Burdock and Dandelion Beer

This is made by using the burdock beer recipe but substituting dandelion roots for part of the root weight. Dandelion roots give a rather bitter taste so about half and half is ideal.

Lesser Burdock *Arctium minus* Bernh. A biennial herb found throughout the British Isles except in the Scottish Highlands, burdock occurs on waste places, waysides, scrub and woodland margins. It flowers from July to September.

The English name indicates a bur-bearing fruit of the plant and the large dock-like leaves. Matthew Robinson in *The New Family Herbal* says of burdock, 'It is so well known, even by little boys, who pull off the bur to throw and stick upon one another'. Burdock was used in early times for the treatment of leprosy and has always been considered one of the finest blood purifiers. It is still used in modern drugs for the treatment of digestive troubles and skin diseases. The roots, stems and leaves of burdock can be eaten raw or boiled and it is cultivated as a vegetable in Japan, while in the Midlands burdock beer is still popular. The young leaf stems can be collected from May onwards, the leaves picked in June and July, and the roots dug any time during the autumn. The hard outer peel of the stems should be removed to leave the soft, moist core.

To collect burdock roots you will need a good spade as they can go down very deep and if you collect them in a gravelly area as I do it will be hard work. As you will see from the photograph, I first tackled burdock in the summer when the plants initially appear but really it is best to gather the year-old roots in the autumn, after they have stored up their goodness to last through the winter.

Boiled Burdock Stems

Use the young shoots, leaf stems and flower stalks. Peel to leave only the soft core, and chop. Boil for 6-10 minutes in as little water as possible. Drain well and serve with melted butter and freshly ground black pepper.

Burdock Boiled Dry

Cut burdock roots into long thin pieces the size of matchsticks. Place in an open, heavy pan and cover with water, adding a good dash of soy sauce and a small pinch of salt. Simmer for 15 minutes and then allow the juices to evaporate so the soy sauce flavour is absorbed in the cooked roots, but make sure it does not catch. The flavour of the burdock pieces will be strong but worth the trouble.

Daisies. Photographed June 1 (very blue photograph as it was late in the evening).

Daisy Bellis perennis L. Very common on grassland, lawns and roadsides, it is found from early spring onwards. The leaves can be eaten in salads but they are rather tough so make sure to pick fresh, young ones.

Pignut salad flavoured with wall pepper. Photographed in the Yorkshire Dales, June 16.

The pignut plant in flower. Photographed June 16.

Pignut *Conopodium majus* (Gouan) Loret. A perennial herb generally distributed throughout the British Isles, it is found in fields and woods and flowers from May to July. In some soils the pignuts may be obtained by pulling on the root that leads down to the tuber, but in most soils the roots break off very quickly and must be unearthed with a knife and carefully traced down to the tuber.

Pechey, in 1694, reported that 'Our Country-people eat the Root raw; but when it is pill'd and boyl'd in fresh Broth, with a little Peper, it is pleasant Food, and very nourishing.' Caliban, in *The Tempest*, promises:

I prithee, let me bring thee where crabs grow;
And I with my long nails will dig thee pig-nuts.

Country children used to fill the gaps between meals by chewing pignuts on their way to and from school.

Before eating raw, each nut needs to be peeled or scraped clean.

Pignut and Grapefruit Salad

SERVES TWO
1 large grapefruit, 1 apple
10 pignuts
A small bunch of wall pepper
Juice of ½ a lemon

Peel and de-pith the grapefruit, cutting each segment into 3, and cut the apple into similar sized pieces. Clean and peel the pignuts and cut in half. Flavour with small pieces of wall pepper and mix together with the lemon juice. No pepper or salt is needed on this dish, which can be served as a starter or as a fruit salad to sharpen the palate after a rich meal.

Wall Pepper *Sedum acre* L. A common native perennial, found on walls, roofs, rocks and shingle; it flowers from June to July.

It has a strong, acrid, peppery taste and may be added to salads to give sharpness. I tried it in my pignut salad and found it super.

Fireweed or **Rosebay Willow-Herb** *Chamaenerion augustifolium* (L.) Scop. Rosebay was once a rare native species but it began to spread in the middle of the nineteenth century and is now common throughout Britain. The seeds must be subjected to high ` temperatures before they can germinate and therefore often spring up on recently burnt ground or, as in the Second World War, on blitzed land, hence the names Fireweed and Bomb-site plant.

The name willow-herb refers to the leaf shape, similar to the narrow leaves of the willow. The leaves are also similar to those of the bay tree, while the flowers are rose-coloured, hence rosebay.

Most parts of the plant can be used. The roots, dug up in spring, may be boiled as a vegetable or added to casseroles. The young shoots should be collected in late spring, peeled, and eaten like asparagus, either boiled or baked in butter. In the Gaspe Peninsula, the French Canadians call the herb 'wild asparagus'. The leaves and shoots together may be used as a pot-herb, while the leaves themselves may be used as a salad or vegetable or as a substitute and adulterant of tea.

The herb is still popular as a vegetable in certain countries in Europe, especially Russia where it is used to make Kaporie tea. In

Wall pepper growing in its typical habitat. Photographed June 17.

Rosebay willow-herb as a food is a non-starter for me. Photographed in Scotland, July 25.

British Columbia, the Indians peel the stalks and eat the gelatinous pith fresh or cook it as a soup, while some tribes use the core as a flour for bread-making. Finally, the shoots may be used to make a beer-like liquid which, in certain parts of Siberia, is mixed with the hallucinogenic juice of the fly agaric fungus (*Amanita muscaria*). This produces a brew the effects of which are said to be comparable to the combined effects of gin and LSD!

Despite all these exotic tales of eating rosebay willow-herb I have been unable to make it palatable. It is far too bitter to enjoy as any kind of vegetable.

Tansy with apples and tansy pancakes in the garden of a cottage in Honey Pot Lane, Suffolk. Photographed July 8.

Tansy *Chrysanthemum vulgare* (L.) Bernh. Tansy is a perennial, common throughout the British Isles and occurring along roadsides, hedgerows and waste places. It flowers from July to September.

The name 'tansy' is said to be derived from the Greek word *athanasia*, meaning immortality, which was contracted to 'thansa'. Several reasons are suggested. The plant provides an everlasting flower when dried. The gods are said to have given tansy to Ganymede to make him immortal. During the Middle Ages tansy cakes were largely eaten to offset the effects of the limited fare of Lent. There was a widely held belief that fish, which was eaten during Lent, somehow encouraged worms in people and tansy was used medicinally to get rid of worms. Tansy puddings were made for much the same purpose although eaten by the more aristocratic medieval community.

John Gerard, in his 17th-century *Herball*, explains their effect: 'In the Spring time are made with the leaves here of newly sprung up, and with eggs, cakes of Tansies, which be pleasant in taste, and good for the stomacke. For if any bad humours cleave there unto, it doth perfectly concot them, and scowre them downewards.' During the course of time, the original purpose of tansy cakes was lost and they came to be eaten symbolically on Easter Day to commemorate the bitter herbs eaten at the Jewish Passover.

On Easter Sunday be the pudding seen,
To which the tansy lends her sober green.

Tansy cakes became a part of many Easter traditions.

At Trinity College, Cambridge, tansies were eaten on Easter Monday and Tuesday. They were often given as prizes at Easter sports, including a traditional match where archbishops and bishops played handball with men of their congregation. At Chester, the bishop and dean are said to have taken eggs into the cathedral and, at certain stages of the service, to have engaged in an egg-throwing match with the choristers. Following this, they all retired to dine on gammon and tansy pudding. Tansy has been much cultivated as a medicinal and pot-herb and was once found in every cottage garden. It was valued as a substitute for the then expensive spices, nutmeg and cinnamon. It was used to flavour custards, milk puddings, cakes, omelettes and freshwater fish and in Ireland it flavoured locally-made sausages known as 'drisheens', In Sussex, tansy leaves were worn in the shoes to prevent the ague. Tansy is one of the most written about plants in the ancient herbals, and the general consensus of opinion is that it was used at Easter to purify the blood after Lent. However, this is impossible in England as the plant only begins to develop leaves at the end of May and even the changing of the date of Easter cannot account for this. Anyway, timing aside, the taste of the leaves is strong, pungent and quite disgusting; it is only added to the dishes for its traditional, medicinal qualities. Having said this I am including one of the ancient recipes for interest and also two modern recipes which do work. It was also claimed that tansy was used as a flavouring for roast lamb, similar to the way we use mint today.

A Tansy

SERVES FOUR
2 eggs
1½ dl (5 fl oz) double cream
1 thick slice of white bread, made into breadcrumbs
2 teaspoons finely chopped tansy
½ teaspoon grated nutmeg
¼ teaspoon grated lemon rind
3 eating apples
25 g (1 oz) butter

Mix together eggs, cream, breadcrumbs, tansy, nutmeg and lemon rind. Allow to stand for 10 minutes. Peel, core and slice apples. Melt the butter in a frying pan, add apples and cook gently for 5 minutes or until tender. Pour egg mixture over the apples and cook over a low heat for a further ten minutes or until almost firm. Do not stir the mixture. When firm, remove the pan from the heat and place under a pre-heated grill until golden brown. Cut into slices, sprinkle with sugar and serve immediately.

Tansy just coming into flower on the roadside. Photographed July 8.

Tansy Pancakes

SERVES FOUR
50 g (2 oz) plain flour
3 eggs
1½ dl (5 fl oz) double cream
1 tablespoon sugar
4 macaroons, crumbled
½ teaspoon grated orange rind
2 teaspoons chopped fresh tansy
2 tablespoons sherry
1 tablespoon melted butter
50 g (2 oz) butter

Sift flour into a basin, gradually beat in eggs and cream to form a smooth batter. Add the sugar, macaroons, orange rind, tansy, sherry and melted butter and mix until thoroughly combined. Set aside for 30 minutes.

Melt butter in a frying pan. When hot, add 2 tablespoons of batter and cook over a moderate heat for 2-3 minutes, turning pancakes to brown on both sides. Repeat the process with each pancake. Serve immediately with sugar and slices of orange.

A Tansy

'Take three pints of Cream, fourteen New-laid-eggs (seven whites put away) one pint of juyce of Spinage, six or seven spoonfuls of juyce of Tansy, a Nutmeg (or two) sliced small, half a pound of sugar, and a little salt. Beat all these well together, then fry it in a pan with no more Butter than is necessary. When it is enough, serbe it up with the juyce of Orange or slices of Limon upon it.'

This amazing recipe from Sir Kenelme Digbie, 1669, when reduced to 3 eggs, made a sort of watery omelette which was just palatable served with the orange juice.

Chamomile flowers drying in the sun. Photographed June 26.

Chamomile *Chamaemelum nobile* (L.) All. Chamomile is found throughout England, Wales and Ireland, but is less common in Scotland, on sandy commons, pastures and grassy roadsides. It flowers in June and July.

The true chamomile can be distinguished from the mayweeds and feverfews by its sweet scent, reminiscent of apples. From this it derives its generic name, literally 'earth-apple', from the Greek *kamai*, on the ground, and *melon*, apple. The Spaniards call the plant 'Manzanilla', meaning 'a little apple', and they have also given this name to one of their lightest sherries which is flavoured with the plant. The specific name, *nobilis*, denotes the many healing virtues of the plant. The Egyptians believed that it cured ague and for this reason dedicated it to their gods.

Chamomile tea has a soothing, sedative effect which is absolutely harmless and considered a certain remedy for nightmares. It is said to be a 'herb doctor' with the power of reviving any wilting plant placed near it and is also reputed to grow better for being trampled, giving rise to the following proverb: 'As the herb chamomile the more it is trodden down the more is spreadeth abroad, so virtue and honesty the more it is spiteth the more it sprouteth'. For use as a tea, the flowerheads should be gathered just as the petals begin to turn down.

Chamomile Tea

Take one teaspoon of fresh or dried flowers per cup and steep in boiling water for 3 or 4 minutes, then strain. I prefer to drink it flavoured with a little honey or sugar.

Lime tea has the most delicious, subtle, greeny gold colour. Photographed June 29.

Lime *Tilia europaea* L. The lime tree is introduced throughout Britain. It is deciduous and has been widely planted over a long period, especially in copses, parks, gardens and roadsides. It flowers in June or early July.

The flowers are used to make linden tea which is famous for its delicious taste and soothing effect on the digestive and nervous system. Honey from lime flowers is regarded as the best flavoured and most valuable in the world and is used extensively in medicine and liqueurs. The leaves exude a saccharine matter with the same composition as the manna of Mount Sinai and the sap has been used to make sugar. During the last century, Missa, a French chemist, found that the fruit of the lime, ground up with some of

the flowers in a mortar, furnished a substance much resembling chocolate in flavour.

The flowers, including the wing-like bracts, should be used in late June or July, gathered while in full bloom and laid out on trays in a warm, well-ventilated room for two to three weeks.

Lime or Linden Tea

Infuse one teaspoon of dried lime flowers in one cup of water for 5–10 minutes, strain and drink as it comes or with a few grains of sugar. Lime tea has a lovely, honey-like scent and is said to be soothing to the digestion and nerves so it is often taken last thing at night to help induce sleep.

Majoram jelly is an excellent adjunct to cold ham. Photographed in the Chiltern Hills, where it can be found in profusion, July 22.

Pine needles can make a refreshing tea. Photographed June 20.

Wild Marjoram *Origanum vulgare* L. Marjoram is common in England and Wales, local in Scotland extending to Caithness, and common in southern Ireland. It grows in dry pastures, hedge-banks and scrub, usually on calcerous soil. It is perennial and flowers from July to October.

The generic name, *Origanum,* is derived from the Greek *oros,* a mountain, and *ganos,* joy, an allusion to the gay appearance of these plants growing on hillsides. The ancient Greeks believed that marjoram growing on a grave foretold the happiness of the departed soul, while young couples were customarily crowned with the herb. In Kent, marjoram was used to make tea and large quantities gathered for this purpose were hung in the cottages to dry. It has also been used to flavour ale. The old 16th-century *Lustgarten der Gesundjheit* gives a recipe for wild marjoram sugar, the chopped buds and flowers being added to a jar of sugar which then stood in the sun for 24 hours. A small quantity of the sugar taken over a period of two or three days was claimed to cure diseases of the kidneys and eyes. This aromatic sugar is a delicious addition to cakes and desserts.

Marjoram Jelly

2 kg (4 lb) cooking apples
6 dl (1 pint) water
Sugar
1½ dl (¼ pint) white vinegar
Large bunch of marjoram

Wash the apples and drain well. Cut them into pieces without peeling or coring then put into a preserving pan with the vinegar and water. Reserve one quarter of the marjoram and add the rest to the apples. Simmer for about 45 minutes until the apples are soft and pulpy. Strain through a jelly bag but do not squeeze the pulp

or the jelly will be cloudy. Measure the juice and allow 450 g (1 lb) sugar to each pint. Heat the juice gently, stirring in the sugar until dissolved. Boil hard to setting point, which will take 10-15 minutes. Chop the remaining marjoram leaves finely and stir into the pan. Leave to stand off the heat for 5 minutes and then stir well to distribute the herb leaves. Pour into small, hot, sterilized jars and cover. Serve with pork, ham or poultry.

This delicious recipe comes from Mary Norwak.

Marjoram in Salads

Finely chopped marjoram is excellent used as a garnish on tomato or potato salad and I like it mixed with mint and added to any kind of green salad.

Pine *Pinus sylvestris* L. This evergreen, the dominant tree of considerable areas in Scotland, is also found on sandy soils in south-east England, It flowers in May and June.

A clump of pine trees in a conspicuous position near a dwelling is traditionally supposed to have been planted as a sign to fugitive Jacobites that they would find safe harbour there.

Pine Needle Tea

Use the fresh green pine needles, allowing 2 teaspoons per cup. Bruise the needles before pouring boiling water on them. Stir and allow to infuse for 5-10 minutes. Strain and serve without milk. This can be sweetened with honey or a little sugar if desired.

Wild strawberries really repay the effort of searching for them. Photographed August 2.

Wild Strawberry *Fragaria vesca* L. A perennial herb common throughout the British Isles, it occurs in woods and scrub on base-rich soils and on basic grassland, sometimes becoming locally dominant in woods and on calcareous soils. The wild strawberry flowers from April to July and the fruits are borne from late June until August.

The wild strawberry has a flavour and fragrance more delicate than that of the cultivated variety but today it is much more commonly used in France than in Britain. The name derives from the Anglo-Saxon 'streow berie', literally a straying plant that bears berries, alluding to the runners which stray from the parent plant in all directions.

As early as 200 BC, strawberries were cultivated by the Romans and this practice was first recorded in Britain during the 14th century. The fruit was also known as 'hautbois':

> *Here strawberries, the best,*
> *Nice hautboys fresh and fine;*
> *With cream by all confest,*
> *Delicious vespertine.*

Dr Losch, in *Les Plantes Médicinales,* gives some delicious ways of serving *fraises de bois:* with sugar, wine, cream, orange juice, champagne or vinegar.

For medicinal purposes, the leaves were frequently used in the past for various 'spring drinks' which were taken, with ground ivy, to stimulate the system after a winter diet that would, by our standards, have been deficient in vitamins and mineral salts. Matthew Robinson in *The New Family Herbal* says: 'they are good even for the teeth, and may be used as a safe and effectual dentifrice', and also 'they take away redness of the face spots'.

The cultivated strawberries that we find in the shops have not been bred from the European wild strawberry but from wild American species, although you may occasionally find a cultivated form of the wild strawbery known as Alpine strawberry.

Strawberries and Cream

It is extremely difficult to pick wild strawberries in any kind of quantity but if you take the trouble they are well worthwhile. Toss the fruit with a dash of Kirsch and a sprinkle of castor sugar, leave

for an hour or so to soak up the flavour and then serve with fresh cream.

This recipe comes from Sir Kenelme Digbie, 1669, and I quote it for interest only. As far as I am concerned I prefer to eat all the wild strawberries I find fresh or with cream.

Wild Cherry *Prunus avium* L. A deciduous tree, rather common in England, Wales and Ireland but becoming rare in northern Scotland, it is found in woods and hedges. It flowers in late April or May and the fruit ripens in early July. It can be substituted for cultivated cherries in any recipe but the amount of sugar must be adjusted to compensate, as the wild crop is normally very sour.

The cherry is quite common in folklore. It is strangely mixed up with the cuckoo, probably due to the tradition that the cuckoo must eat three good meals of cherries before he is allowed to stop singing. Buckinghamshire children would recite the following rhyme while shaking a blossoming cherry tree:

> *Cuckoo, cherry tree,*
> *Good bird tell me,*
> *How many years before I die.*

The next burst of calling from the cuckoo was supposed to provide the answer. An old proverb predicts the nature of the coming year as follows:

> *A cherry year's a merry year;*
> *A sloe year's a woe year;*
> *A haw year's a braw year:*
> *An apple year's a drappin' year;*
> *A plum year's a glum year.*

The well-known saying 'all or nothing' is also expressed 'the whole tree or not a cherry on it', while to 'make two bites of a cherry' is to divide something too small to be worth dividing.

In Switzerland and Germany the spirit, *kirschwasser,* is distilled from wild cherries. The gum of the tree may also be eaten and is reputed to have kept a hundred men alive for two months during a siege.

Wild Cherry Brandy

Take a big jar with a good sealing top and half fill with cherries.

Wild cherries. Unfortunately, you have to pick them before they are really ripe, otherwise the birds will get them all. Photographed July 10.

Add 6 blanched almonds and 225 g (8 oz) castor sugar and top up the jar with brandy. Screw down the lid and shake thoroughly. Every time you pass the jar, reverse it. After 3 months, strain and bottle the liqueur.

Wild Cherry Soup

SERVES FOUR
450 g (1 lb) stoned cherries – keep the stones
3 dl (½ pint) water
2.5 cm (1 in) cinnamon bark
3 dl (½ pint) red wine, preferably home-made
Zest of one lemon, a little dried, mashed potato

Put cherries, water, cinnamon and lemon zest in a saucepan and cook fast for 10 minutes. Process the lot through a blender and add the red wine which has been boiled with the crushed cherry stones and strained. Thicken this to taste with dried, mashed potato. Sweeten as necessary and serve at once.

Both the above recipes reproduced by permission of the Hamlyn Publishing Group Ltd from *The Second Country Book* edited by Barbara Hargreaves.

Cherry Wine

4½ litres (1 gallon) water
1½ kg (3 lb) sugar
1½ kg (3 lb) cherries
2 lemons
2 teaspoons yeast

Pick the cherries when really ripe and de-stalk. If you cannot find enough add shop fruit but remember that this will make a much sweeter wine. Place in a bucket, boil three-quarters of the water and pour over the fruit. When it cools mash up the fruit with your hands. Allow to stand for three days, then squeeze the fruit through a wine bag. Make up the sugar syrup with the last quarter of the water, then put into a fermentation jar. Grate lemon rind and squeeze juice, then make up yeast starter and add to the wine. Seal with a cotton wool bung and leave to stand for three days. Now place on airlock and allow to ferment for three months, then syphon into clean jar and keep for another 3 or 4 months when it will be ready to drink.

This recipe was given to me by Jeff and Jenny Stone. It makes a delicious, sharp, dry wine.

Eryngoes. A very traditional sweetmeat; alas, now too rare a plant to be dug up. Photographed September 20.

Sea holly *Eryngium maritimum* L. This perennial occurs around the coasts of the British Isles north to Shetland, excepting the east coast north of Flamborough Head. It is found on sandy and shingly shores and flowers from July to August.

The generic name is derived from the Greek *eruggarein*, to eructate, and refers to the plants supposed efficacy in flatulent disorders. The roots, which resemble chestnuts in taste, may be eaten boiled or roasted or used to make jelly, but they are more commonly candied as 'eryngoes' or the 'kissing comfits' alluded to by Falstaff. These sweetmeats used to be obtainable in London shops.

I include this plant because of its historical importance but, in fact, it should not be dug up except in exceptional circumstances.

Candied Eryngoes

'The manner to condite Eryngoes. Refine sugar fit for the purpose, and take a pound of it, the white of an egge, and a pint of cleere water, boile them together and scum it, then let it boile until it be come to good strong syrup, and when it is boiled, as it cooleth, adde thereto a saucer full of Rose-water, a spoone full of Cinnamon water, and a graine of Muske, which have been infused together the night before, and now strained; into which syrup being more than halfe cold, put in your roots to soke and infuse until the next day; your roots being ordered in manner hereafter following:

These your roots being washed and picked, must be boiled in faire water by the space of foure houres, until they be soft, then must they be pilled cleane, as ye pill parsneps, and the pith must bee drawne out at the end of the root; and if there be any whose pith cannot be drawne out at the end, then you must split them, and so take out the pith: these you must also keepe from much handling, that they may be cleane, let them remaine in the syrup till the next day, and then set them on the fire in a faire broad pan until they be verie hot, but let them not boile at all: let them there remaine over the fire an houre or more, removing them easily in the pan from one place to another with a wooden slice. This done, have in readinesse great cap or royall papers, whereupon you must strew some sugar, upon which lay your roots after that you have taken them out of the pan. These papers you must put into a Stove, or hot house to harden; but if you have not such a place, lay them before a

good fire. In this manner if you condite your roots, there is not any that can prescribe you a better way. And thus may you condite any other root whatsoever, which will not onely bee exceeding delicate, but very wholesome, and effectuall against the diseases above named.'

This recipe comes from John Gerard's *Herball*, 1633. The roots take on the delicate flavour of the rose water.

Dulse *Palmaria palmata* (L.) Kuntze. Common around our coasts on the middle shore between the tides, dulse grows on rocks and on the stems of oar weed. It can be found from spring to autumn and the beautiful, dark red fronds can be rich in potassium and magnesium.

Dulse Vegetable

The Carswells had this to say in their *Scottish Wayfarers' Book*, 1936:

'To cook Dulse, wash carefully and simmer in fresh water until tender. Strain, cut up small, heat through in a pan with butter, add pepper and salt and offer it to those who really love you. They are the only people, yourself excepted, who are likely to eat it.'

I hope your friends may be more enlightened and also try it because, like most seaweeds, it is extremely nutritious. It can be eaten raw or served finely chopped with potatoes or cottage cheese.

Cucumber and Seaweed Salad

SERVES FOUR
80 g (3½ oz) dulse
1 cucumber
4 tablespoons vinegar
3 tablespoons dark soy sauce
1 teaspoon sugar
Salt

Wash dulse and pat dry with a clean cloth, then cut into 4 cm (1½ in) lengths. Mix together the vinegar, soy sauce, sugar and salt. Combine the cucumber and dulse in a salad bowl and pour the vinegar dressing over it. Mix gently and serve.

This recipe is adapted from Peter and Joan Martin's *Japanese Cooking.*

Dulse grows on rocks between the tide marks. Photographed July 15.

Dulse Hash

SERVES TWO

450 g (1 lb) potatoes
1 teaspoon mustard seeds
2 tablespoons olive oil
2 cloves of garlic, crushed
4 chopped mushrooms
1 small onion, chopped
1 sweet red pepper
25 g (1 oz) dried dulse, torn into bite-sized pieces
A sprinkle of cayenne pepper and paprika

Wash the potatoes and partially cook in boiling water. Allow them
to cool, then peel and cut into cubes. In a heavy frying pan heat oil
and when hot add mustard seeds and potatoes. Fry until pale gold
and then remove the potatoes from the pan. Reheat the pan and
stir-fry the garlic, mushrooms, onion and red pepper for 5 minutes.
Add the dulse and potatoes and continue cooking, stirring
constantly for 10 minutes. When it is nearly cooked, add a sprinkle
of cayenne pepper and paprika. If you have a penchant for hot
curries add extra cayenne pepper to taste.

This is an excellent American recipe which I have adapted from
Cooking with Sea Vegetables by Sharon Ann Rhoads, published by
Autumn Press Inc.

Dulse Croquettes

MAKES EIGHT CROQUETTES

100 g (4 oz) rolled oats
25 g (1 oz) finely chopped dried dulse
225 g (8 oz) each of parsnips and carrots
2 tablespoons olive oil

Boil the parsnips and carrots until tender, drain and reserve some
of the water. Mash the parsnips and carrots together, adding a little
water if necessary to make a smooth paste.

In a bowl combine the oats and dulse. Add a quarter of this
mixture to the vegetable paste and mix well together. Form into
croquettes and roll in oats and dulse to coat the surface. Chill for 20
minutes before cooking.

Heat the oil in a frying pan and sauté the croquettes over a low
heat for 5 minutes on each side, until heated through and crisp, or
bake at 180°C (350°F, Mark 4) for 20 minutes.

Dulse croquettes make an excellent starter or they can be served
as a vegetable with roast lamb.

Carragheen soup is delicious, rich and nourishing. As you can imagine this photograph ended in disaster – all my ingredients were washed away!
Photographed at Ballyandreen, in Ireland, August 1.

Carragheen mousse, both the sweet and the savoury versions. Photographed July 15.

Carragheen or **Irish Moss** *Chondrus crispus* Lyngb. The branched fronds are up to 15 cm (6 in) long, reddish purple in colour but they may bleach white or show green tints when exposed to strong light. It can be found on most of our rocky coasts but is most common in Ireland and Cornwall, on rocks on the lower shore in spring or summer. There is another seaweed that is very similar in appearance, batter frond *Gigartina stellata* Batt. Batter frond differs in that it has a concave surface so that the sides of each segment tend to inroll and also its older specimens have tiny pimples.

Carragheen can be used fresh or dried to make a sort of gelatine which has been used traditionally in Ireland, America, Iceland and the coasts of northern France. It is high in vitamin A and iodine and it also contains vitamin B and many minerals. In Ireland, children are given blancmange made with carragheen, sometimes flavoured with chocolate or coffee.

Carragheen Soup

SERVES FOUR
2 dl (1 cup) dried carragheen
3 slices lean bacon
450 g (1 lb) carrots
3 sticks of celery
1 litre (2 pints) water
Pepper and salt, thyme

First soak the dried carragheen for about 15 minutes then pick out any bits of grit or very dry ends. Discard the waste, chop all the ingredients into small pieces and add to the water. Boil for 45 minutes and then liquidize, check the flavour and add salt and pepper if necessary.

This makes a delicious and nourishing soup because the carragheen gives it a thick body which creates a most pleasant texture. This is only a basic recipe; carragheen may be added to any soup or stew to thicken and enrich it.

Carragheen Sweet Mousse

SERVES FOUR
6 g (¼ oz) dried carragheen
6 dl (1 pint) milk
2 strips lemon rind
12 g (½ oz) sugar
1 egg
Fresh raspberries to decorate

Soak the dried carragheen for 15 minutes in water, then pick out the grit or dried ends and discard the water. Add the carragheen and lemon peel to the milk, slowly bring to the boil and then simmer for about 10 minutes or until the mixture is quite thick. Separate the yolk from the egg white and beat the yolk with the sugar. Strain in the carragheen mixture, stirring well. Fold in the stiffly beaten egg white and pour into individual dishes or into a nice fluted mould. Turn out when set in 2-3 hours.

This makes a very nice mousse which is lovely on its own but even better when served with stewed fruit. If you leave out the eggs the mixture will set just as well and make a nourishing blancmange, rather plain on its own but excellent with stewed fruit, topped with a little cream.

Carragheen and Mackerel Savoury Mousse

SERVES FOUR
225 g (8 oz) smoked mackerel
6 g (¼ oz) carragheen
3 dl (½ pint) water
6 dl (1 pint) milk
2 strips lemon rind
1 egg
Pepper and salt
Fennel, lemon and black olives to decorate

Soak dried carragheen in water for 15 minutes, remove any grit or dried ends and discard the water. Add together the lemon rind, the carragheen, the milk and the water. Bring to the boil and simmer gently for about 25 minutes until the milk is really thick. Separate the egg yolk from the white, beat the yolk and add it to the strained milk and carragheen. Break the smoked mackerel into little pieces and add to the mixture. Flavour to taste with pepper and salt. Beat the egg white until it is stiff and then fold into the egg yolk mixture. Pour into a damp mould, leave 2-3 hours to set, then turn out and decorate with fennel, lemon slices and black olives.

I love chicken stuffing made with thyme, especially when it cooks to a stiff consistency that can be carved. Photographed July 15.

Wild Thyme *Thymus drucei* Ronn. or *Thymus serpyllum* agg. Wild thyme is common throughout the British Isles on dry grasslands, heaths, dunes, screes and among rocks. It flowers from May until August.

Thyme is my favourite herb. It makes an excellent addition to roasting meat – chicken, heart and especially liver – and gives a nice strong flavour to a herb omelette. Most mushroom dishes benefit from it, as do salad dressings and vinegar. Wild thyme when found in Britain is rather mild in flavour compared with cultivated forms, or indeed, with the wild thyme found around the Mediterranean, so remember to be lavish with it. A tea can be made with the leaves of thyme which is good for colds and throat complaints.

Thyme has been traditionally associated with bravery and courage. Roman soldiers used to bathe in water infused with thyme before going into battle. Thyme can be dried and stored with very little loss of flavour.

Herb Butter

1 heaped teaspoon of thyme and parsley mixed
50 g (2 oz) butter

Take thyme and parsley, chop finely then blend them together with the butter using a palette knife. With your fingers make into a rough sausage shape 2½ cm (1 in) thick, wrap in foil and then roll between two boards to make a good, even sausage shape. Refrigerate so that it will become hard and can be cut into slices. Use as a finishing touch on steak, chops or chicken portions.

Thyme is an important ingredient in herb butter and in bouquet garni. Photographed July 15.

Bouquet Garni

Thyme
Bay leaves
Peppercorns
Parsley
Muslin, cotton

For each bouquet cut a 10 cm (4 in) square from the muslin. Take a good sprig of thyme and parsley, one bay leaf, two peppercorns and place them on the square of muslin. Pull up the sides and tie the small bundle with cotton leaving the ends long so that you can hang them over the edge of the pan, then the bouquet can be easily removed before serving.

Thyme and Sour Cream Dressing

1 dl (4 fl oz) sour cream
1 tablespoon olive oil
2 tablespoons thyme
Pepper and salt
1 teaspoon lemon juice
Garlic

Chop the thyme as finely as you can, then mix together in a jar with the olive oil, lemon juice and a squeeze of garlic. Shake well so that the oil breaks up and emulsifies with the lemon juice, then stir into the sour cream and flavour with pepper and salt.

This makes a gorgeous dressing, especially for things like beetroot, cucumber, carrot or any kind of bean salad.

Thyme and Parsley Stuffing

1 small onion
100 g (4 oz) fresh breadcrumbs
2 rashers of bacon
1 tablespoon shredded suet
1 tablespoon chopped parsley
1 tablespoon chopped thyme
1 egg, 1 lemon
Pepper and salt

Finely chop the onion and bacon and lightly fry them together.

Wild basil growing in a disused chalk pit. Photographed July 29.

Prepare the bowl of breadcrumbs yourself (bought ones are no good) and add the suet, bacon, onion, finely chopped thyme, parsley, pepper, salt, the juice of ½ the lemon and a little grated rind. Lightly beat the egg and mix it into the mixture to bind it.

This is an ideal stuffing for chicken or turkey. When my mother, Elsie, makes it, she stuffs the neck end of the bird and sews it in. It then expands a bit and cooks solid so that it can be carved in thin slices.

Wild Basil *Clinopodium vulgare* . A native plant that is common in England, uncommon in Scotland and very rare in Ireland. It is found in scrub and hedges especially on chalk or limestone. Wild basil can be used fresh with salads and is especially good with tomatoes. It can be dried and kept for use in stews and soups. The flavour is rather mild so your salad will need a liberal quantity of chopped young leaves.

91

Raspberry wine. Photographed near Bridge of Alford, Scotland, August 15.

Wild Raspberry *Rubus idaeus* L. A perennial with woody, biennial stems, common throughout the British Isles in woods and heaths, especially in hilly districts, it flowers from June to August and bears fruit from July to September.

The specific name *idaeus* was given to the raspberry by Dioscorides because of its abundance on Mount Ida in Asia Minor. Traditionally the village midwife encouraged her patients to drink an infusion of raspberry leaves to make childbirth easier but, as time went on, this old-fashioned aid was largely superseded by imported drugs. However, when these were unobtainable at the beginning of the Second World War, research was carried out and it was discovered that raspberry-leaf tea was no 'old wives' tale' but contained a valuable principle, fragarine, which acted very beneficially on the pelvic muscles of the mother at childbirth.

Raspberry vinegar is an acid syrup made with the fruit juice, sugar and white wine vinegar. This, with water added, makes an excellent, cooling drink in summer.

Raspberry Wine

750 g (1½ lb) raspberries
1 kg (2.2 lb) sugar
2 oranges
Yeast
2 campden tablets
4½ litres (1 gallon) water

Pick over the raspberries, removing any unripe fruit and place in a plastic bucket. Pour over it 3 litres (5 pints) of boiling water, then mash the fruit up well with a wooden spoon and add one crushed campden tablet. Leave for 2 days then strain off the juice through a muslin, pressing well to get all the fruit juice through. Add the juice of the oranges. Boil up the rest of the water with the sugar and add it to the liquid. Start the yeast and add it when the mixture is cool enough. Leave to ferment in the bucket for 3 days, then move to a fermenting jar with an airlock. Leave to ferment until all working has stopped, filter and add a crushed campden tablet. Taste it. It may be too dry; if so you can sweeten it with a very small amount of sugar syrup. Bottle in sterilized bottles and store in a cool place.

This is a really special wine with a sharp, distinct flavour, ideal for drinking after a meal. I have found that it is delicious as soon as it has finished working and I have never kept any more than a few months, but as far as I can tell it does not improve with age.

Wild raspberries. Photographed August 15.

Yarrow tea is amazingly good. Photographed October 10.

Raspberry Vinegar

1.2 litres (2 pints) fresh raspberries
6 dl (1 pint) white vinegar
Sugar

Bruise the raspberries with a wooden spoon and pour over the vinegar, stirring well. Cover and stir every day for 4-5 days. Strain through a jelly bag. For every 3 dl (½ pint) of liquid add 1½ dl of sugar. Heat to just below boiling temperature for 10-15 minutes. (If it does come to the boil you will lose the bright red colour but otherwise there is no ill effect.) Bottle when cold using stoppered bottles. Dilute in a proportion of about 1 part vinegar to 5 parts lemonade and serve on hot, summer days. Excellent for a cold when diluted with hot water.

From Lyndsay Shearer, out of May Buchan's *Common Place Book*.

Yarrow *Achillea millefolium* L. Yarrow is a perennial, common on all but the poorest soils throughout the British Isles. It occurs in meadows, pastures, grassy banks, hedgerows and waysides and flowers from June to October. The whole plant is used and can be collected from May to November.

The generic name is derived from the Greek warrior Achilles who, during the Trojan War, saved the lives of his warriors by healing their wounds with yarrow. In Sweden yarrow has been used as a substitute for hops in the preparation of beer, to which it was supposed to add an intoxicating effect. Yarrow tea can be brewed as a remedy for severe colds.

To learn the reality of her true love's affection a young girl must pluck yarrow on May eve and place it under her pillow repeating the following rhyme:

> *Good morrow, good morrow, sweet yarrow to thee;*
> *If I see my true love in white, his love to me is ever bright.*
> *If he appears to me in blue, his love to me is ever true.*
> *If he appears to me in black, his love to me will lack.*

Yarrow Tea

Take two or three fresh or dried yarrow leaves per cup of boiling water. Infuse for 4 minutes, strain and serve. Sweeten, if required, with sugar or honey.

I like it served like lemon tea with a slice of lemon and sugar to taste. It is a lovely, soothing drink. Why this tea ever went out of fashion is a mystery to me.

Marsh samphire is superb as a vegetable or pickled to keep for winter. Photographed August 10.

Marsh samphire, the epicurean treat of the salt marshes. Photographed August 10.

Marsh Samphire or **Glasswort** *Salicornia europaea* L. Samphire is found locally on the south-east and west coasts of England, also in coastal areas of Wales, the west coasts of Scotland and the coasts of Ireland. It is an annual, occurring on open, sandy mud in salt marshes and flowering in August and September.

Samphire is rich in soda and formerly was commonly employed in making both soap and glass, thus giving it its alternative common name, glasswort. Traditionally, the plant is said to be ready for picking on the longest day, the healthiest specimens being those which have been washed by every tide. Pick during July and August, at low tide. Samphire should be washed carefully soon after collection and it is best eaten within a few hours but it will keep in the fridge for a day or two. Young plants can be eaten raw, older ones should be cooked in boiling, unsalted water.

Boiled Samphire

Wash the samphire leaving the roots intact, tie in bundles and boil in shallow, unsalted water for 8-10 minutes. Cut the string and serve nice and hot with melted butter and pepper. Each stem contains a woody stalk and the way to eat them is to pick them up by the root and bite lightly on them, pulling the fleshy part from the woody centre. Samphire is a real delicacy and should be tried at the first opportunity.

Pickled Samphire

Marsh samphire may be pickled for winter use. Wash the samphire very thoroughly in fresh water and trim off the roots. Put into a pan and cover with fresh water and add 2 tablespoons of vinegar. Bring slowly to the boil and then boil for 10 minutes. Drain and put into preserving jars. Cover with cold vinegar and seal tightly with vinegar-proof lids. It is ready for use straight away but will keep right through the winter. The samphire must not be over-cooked or it will loose its lovely, bright green colour. It is nicest if pickled in spiced vinegar. This recipe was given to me by Mary Norwak.

Sea pea is found only on Suffolk and Norfolk shingle. Photographed August 29.

This is a very traditional dish which is mentioned in most of the herbals. I put a large jar out when we had a picnic with the British Mycological Society (the mushroom men) and it disappeared down their gullets before you could say 'puff-ball'.

Sea Pea *Lathyrus japonicus* L. Wild. A rare plant, found on the shingle coats of Suffolk and Norfolk, it flowers from June to August and the peas mature between the end of June and the end of August. Bill Pinney, who smokes fish for his own restaurant at Kedgrave in Suffolk, said that the locals eat the little peas. These are the size of lentils and can be eaten raw when young or left on the plant until dry and then picked and used like lentils in stews or soups.

Leg of lamb cooked with mint and mint chutney. Photographed beside Loch Ness August 1.

Apple mint is lovely with drinks. Photographed August 20.

Pennyroyal mint. Note the tiny leaves. Photographed August 26.

Water mint. Photographed August 15.

Corn mint. Photographed August 28.

Mint is said to be named after the nymph Minthe, daughter of Cocytus and favourite of Pluto. Minthe was metamorphosed by Pluto's wife Proserpine, out of jealousy, into the herb called after her:

> *Could Pluto's queen, with jealous fury storm*
> *And Minthe to a fragrant herb transform?*

(Ovid)

Pechey, 1694, says: 'The Smell of it strengthens the brain, and preserves the Memory.'

Water Mint *Mentha aquatica* L. Water mint is a perennial, common throughout the British Isles except in the Scottish Highlands. It is found in swamps, marshes, fens and wet woods, by rivers and ponds and it flowers from July to October.

Corn Mint *Mentha arvensis* L. Almost as common as water mint, it is found in arable fields, woods and damp places, particularly in the south.

Apple Mint *Mentha rotundifolia* L. Huds. Rather rare and only normally found in south-west England, Wales and Ireland, on roadsides and waste places. It is the prettiest of our mints and usually used to decorate summer drinks, especially Pimms.

Pennyroyal *Mentha pulegium* L. This mint used to be fairly common in southern England but unfortunately is now dying out, so if you find it do not massacre the patch. It is rather common in central and southern Europe. The flavour is my favourite amongst the mints.

Mint Chutney

4½ dl (¾ pint) cider vinegar

2 teaspoons mustard powder
2 medium onions
75 g (3 oz) seedless raisins
450 g (1 lb) sugar
450 g (1 lb) eating apples
225 g (8 oz) fresh mint leaves

Put the vinegar into a pan and add the sugar and mustard. Heat gently, stirring well until the sugar has dissolved. Peel the apples and onions and chop very finely. Add to the pan with the finely chopped mint leaves. Bring to the boil and simmer for just 10 minutes. Stir in the raisins and salt and simmer for 5 minutes. Pour into sterilized jars and seal tightly with vinegar-proof lids.

This recipe, by Mary Norwak, is quite delicious.

Mint Sauce

A bunch of mint
1 teaspoon sugar, 4 tablespoons vinegar

Wash the mint and strip off the leaves. Chop finely, then pound them in a pestle and mortar with the sugar. Leave for 30 minutes and then mix with the vinegar and serve. Mint sauce is lovely with lamb or another idea is to insert small bunches of fresh mint into a leg of lamb before cooking.

Mint Tea

In Morocco they serve delicious mint tea without milk but with sugar to taste. To make it, choose a long-leaved, Chinese tea with as green a leaf as you can get. Put slightly less tea than you normally would in the pot, plus a generous bunch of fresh mint and leave to infuse for at least 4 minutes.

97

Summer pudding benefits from the use of wild fruits like bilberries.

Photographed August 25.

Bilberry or **Whortleberry** *Vaccinium myrtillus* L. A deciduous undershrub, common through most of the British Isles, but becoming local in England towards the south-east and absent from several counties in the east and East Midlands. It is found on heaths, moors and woods, and on acid soils, and it flowers from April to June and bears fruit from July to September.

The name 'bilberry' is derived from the Danish *bollebar,* a dark berry. It is also called blaeberry, blueberry, whortleberry and even blackberry. The Irish name for this berry gives its name to one of the most significant days on the Irish calendar, 'Fraughan Sunday', traditionally the Sunday closest to the first day of August. The 'fraughan' is said to be the first of all the wild fruits to ripen and there used to be a special day set aside in the early autumn to go to the hills for a day out, picking fraughans and courting.

In the past, they found a ready market in the bigger towns in Britain and Londoners especially esteemed them in tarts or fresh with cream and a good deal of sweetening. In Yorkshire, bilberry pies were a traditional feature of 'funeral teas'. These pies were simply a mixture of bilberries, sugar and lemon juice baked in a double crust pie. Dorothy Hartley, in *Food in England*, Macdonald & Janes', 1950, says, 'Bilberry Tarts are the best on earth!'

To absorb the juice and give the tarts more substance roast apples were often used at the base of the tart, with the bilberries on top. The fruit is also used in preserves and needs only the smallest quantity of sugar because of the rich juice. If the jam is not intended to be kept, then 225 g (8 oz) of sugar to 450 g (1 lb) of berries is sufficient. Raw, the fruit has a slightly acid flavour but it can be eaten with cream and sugar. In Scotland, the berries are eaten with milk, while the leaves were used as tea, and in the Orkneys a wine of fine flavour was made from the fruit. They are also delicious in pancakes, crumbles and fruit stews. The berries have a high vitamin C content.

Northern Bilberry *Vaccinium uliginosum* L. This species is only found in Scotland but is common in Scandinavia. The berries and leaves have a stronger blue colour.

Blueberry *Vaccinium angustifolium* var. *laevifolium.* The American blueberry, native of the eastern United States of America and Canada, is larger than the British bilberry and can sometimes be seen in our shops.

Summer Pudding

An ever-popular, classic dish that uses soft fruits in season. Here is a recipe using entirely wild fruits.

SERVES SIX

8-10 slices thin, day-old bread
2-3 tablespoons water
100-150 g (4-6 oz) castor sugar
900 g (2 lb) mixed bilberries, raspberries and blackberries,

Rinse a 9 dl (1½ pints) pudding basin with cold water. Trim the crusts from the bread. Cut a circle to fit the bottom of the basin and some wedge-shaped pieces to fit around the sides. Press bread in firmly to line the basin and see that there are no gaps. Reserve a few bread pieces to cover the top.

Place the sugar and water in a saucepan and stir over a low heat to dissolve the sugar. Add the soft fruits and cook for a few minutes only. Remove from the heat and strain off about 1½ dl (¼ pint) of the fruit juices.

Turn the fruit and the rest of the juice into the lined pudding basin and cover the top with remaining bread slices. Stand the basin on a plate to catch any overflowing juices, cover with a saucer and press down with a weight. Leave overnight. Boil up the reserved fruit juices until syrupy and leave until cold. Next day, remove saucer and weight, place a serving plate over the pudding and invert pudding onto plate. Pour over reserved fruit juice. Serve with cream.

This recipe comes from Katie Stewart who suggested trying this traditional recipe with wild fruit. I think the result is superb, better even than when made with the more traditional summer fruits. Remember to use baked rather than steam-baked bread.

Tarte aux myrtilles (bilberries) is a delicious, classic French pastry. Photographed September 1.

Cloudberries are rather rare in Britain but much more plentiful in Scandinavia. Photographed September 5.

Crowberry is quite common on high mountains. Photographed July 20.

Cowberry. Photographed August 25.

Tarte aux Myrtilles

SERVES FOUR-SIX

One of the most delicious French pastries, this recipe involves making a pâte sucrée base covered with a layer of crème patissière, followed by myrtilles (bilberries) and finished off with an apricot glaze.

Pâte Sucrée Base (sweet short pastry):
100 g (4 oz) plain flour, pinch of salt
50 g (2 oz) butter
25 g (1 oz) castor sugar, 1 egg yolk

Sift the flour and salt onto a working surface. Cut the butter up into small cubes. Make a well in the centre of the flour and put in the butter, sugar and egg yolk. Using your fingertips, work the butter, egg and sugar together with the flour until it is all blended. The dough should cling together, leaving the working surface clean so you may have to add a little water as well but do not make it too soft. Knead the dough lightly for about 3 minutes until it forms a smooth ball, then put into a polythene bag and refrigerate for at least 30 minutes before using.

Roll out the pastry to line a 20 cm (8 in) flan tin with a removable base. Cover the base of the flan with greaseproof paper weighed down with baking beans, then bake blind for 10 minutes in a pre-heated oven, 180°C (350°F, Mark 4). Remove beans and greaseproof paper and bake for a further 10 minutes.

Crème Patissière (confectioners' custard):
2 eggs
50 g (2 oz) vanilla sugar
2 tablespoons flour
3 dl (½ pint) milk
25 g (1 oz) unsalted butter

If you don't have any vanilla sugar, add a few drops of vanilla essence to castor sugar. Blend together the eggs, sugar and flour. Bring the milk to the boil and pour onto the egg mixture, stirring continuously. Bring the mixture back to the boil, stirring all the time. Remove from the heat and add the butter. Cover the saucepan with a circle of damp, greaseproof paper and leave the custard until it is cold.

When the pastry is cool, spread a layer of confectioners' custard, ½ cm (¼ in) deep, over the base of the flan. Cover the custard with a generous layer of bilberries then prepare a glaze by sieving apricot jam into a saucepan and heating gently. If it is very thick, thin with a little water, then pour over the layer of bilberries.

I have drawn this recipe largely from *Traditional French Cooking* by Jennie Reekie.

Cowberry Red Bilberry *Vaccinium vitis-idaea* L. Common in the Scottish Highlands, it can also be found in the Pennines. It grows on moors and heaths and is edible but rather tasteless. It is best used to supplement bilberries.

Bilberry Muffins

MAKES TWELVE

350 g (12 oz) sifted plain flour
1½ teaspoons baking powder
¼ teaspoon salt
100 g (4 oz) softened butter
100 g (4 oz) sugar
1 egg
225 g (8 oz) fresh bilberries
1½ dl (¼ pint) milk

Sift together flour, baking powder and salt and set aside. Cream butter, add sugar a little at a time, and continue creaming until mixture is smooth and fluffy. Beat in the egg vigorously, Stir in flour combination and milk, alternating them but beginning and ending with flour. Fold in bilberries and spoon into well-greased patty tins. Bake in a pre-heated oven 200°C (400°F, Mark 6) for 25 to 30 minutes.

This is an American recipe adapted from *The American Heritage Cookbook* by Bullock.

Crowberry *Empetrum nigrum* L. Found on higher areas of moors and mountain ranges in Scotland and northern England. Although sometimes quite plentiful, the berries do not have a very interesting taste and are only worth using to eke out bilberries in a pie or pudding.

Cloudberry *Rubus chamaemorus* L. Found on northern moors and blanket bogs, this species is not normally abundant in Britain but in Scandinavia it can be found in large quantities and is much sought after for jam-making. It has an excellent flavour when fully ripe.

Cranberry *Vaccinium oiycoccus* L. Found in bogs and wet heaths mainly in the Lake District and surrounding area, this is a well-known berry in America and Scandinavia but in Britain one cannot find it in large enough quantities to make the inclusion of special recipes for it worthwhile. The American cranberry is a different plant *Vaccinium macrocarpon* Aiton. with fruit twice the size of the British species.

Autumn, when the fields of stubble are being burned off, is the ideal time for blackberry and apple pie, blackberry jam tarts and a glass of blackberry wine.

Blackberry *Rubus fruticosus* agg. Abundant throughout the British Isles, although less frequent in the Scottish Highlands, it occurs in woods, scrub, hedges and heaths. The blackberry flowers from May to September and bears fruit from August to November. Pick up until early October, after which it tends to get too wet and go mouldy.

There is evidence that blackberries were eaten in England in Neolithic times, for blackberry pips were found in the stomach contents of a Stone Age man dug out of the clay on the Essex coast. A generation ago, blackberry-picking time was an event on the calendar almost as significant as that of Christmas or Easter. Entire families from town and city, armed with buckets and 'tilly' cans, descended on the countryside and plundered the roadsides, hedges, woods and wasteground. There is a taboo against eating blackberries after October 10 because during that night the Devil goes by and spits on every bush. In fact, the fruit does tend to become watery and flavourless at about this time because of the night frosts. The precise choice of date goes back to the period when the English calendar was adjusted by eleven days in 1752. October 10 in the modern calendar corresponds to September 29 in the old calendar, and this is Michaelmas Day, a feast celebrating the primeval war in which St Michael the Archangel hurled Lucifer out of Heaven and down to earth.

Blackberry Wine

Medium dry – makes one gallon:
1½ kg (3 lb) blackberries
2 teaspoons dried baker's yeast
1 lemon
1 kg (2.2 lb) sugar
1 orange
2.2 litres (½ gallon) boiling water

Place blackberries in a large bowl or bucket. Pour on boiling water and mash blackberries with rolling pin or allow to cool then mash by hand. Leave the must for three days and stir daily. Now strain the blackberry must through a wine bag until all juice has been extracted. Make up a sugar syrup with a bag of sugar and 1 litre (1½ pints) of water and boil until the sugar has dissolved. Add the blackberry juice and sugar syrup to jar. Grate the orange and lemon rind, squeeze the juice of the fruits and add this to the gallon jar and make up to 4½ litres (1 gallon) with cooled, boiled water. Add the yeast. Use a cotton wool bung and leave for a few days, then fit an airlock and leave to ferment for at least three months. Syphon into a clean, gallon jar and leave for another six months. It should then be ready to bottle and sample.

Recipe from Jenny Stone. I found that I needed a little pectinol to clear this wine.

Blackberry and Elderberry Wine

Dry
600 g (1¼ lb) blackberries
150 g (5 oz) elderberries
1 kg (2.2 lb) sugar
1 orange
1 lemon
4½ litres (1 gallon) water
Yeast

Pick fruit on a sunny day if possible and remove any leaves or bits and pieces. Do not wash. Put fruit into wine bucket and pour on 2 litres (3-3½ pints) of boiling water, allow to cool, then mash by hand. Allow the must to stand for three days. Stir daily. Strain the wine must through a wine bag to remove all the juice and squeeze pulp as dry as possible. Make up the sugar syrup with the rest of the water. Start the yeast to work, grate lemon and orange rind, squeeze juice of fruit and add all this to wine container. Make up the amount of liquid with cooled, boiled water, add the yeast and seal with cotton wool bung. Leave for two days, then fit an airlock and leave for six months. Syphon into a clean container and keep as long as you can. A very good wine indeed and worth making in large amounts.

Photographed September 5. The recipes are on the following pages.

Dewberries are very similar to blackberries. Photographed September 2.

Dewberry *Rubus caesius* L. Widespread and common, the fruit differs from the ordinary blackberry in that it normally has fewer nodules and is covered in white bloom which gives it a bluish appearance. I personally prefer the flavour to ordinary blackberry.

Blackberry Ale

'Is composed of a strong wort made from two bushels of malt and ¼ lb hops. To this was added the juice of a peck of ripe blackberries and little yeast. After fermentation the cask was stopped up close for six weeks, the ale was then bottled, and was fit to drink at the end of another fortnight.'

From *The Curiosities of Ale and Beer* by John Bickerdyke, 1886.

I have not made this but it sounds interesting!

Bramble Syrup

2½ kg (6 lb) ripe blackberries
Sugar
3 dl (½ pint) water

Wash the fruit well and drain. Put it into a pan with the water and simmer, crushing the fruit frequently with a wooden spoon so that the juices flow. Simmer for about 45 minutes until the fruit has lost its juices, then strain through a jelly bag (muslin or clean tea towel) and measure the juice. Allow 350 g (12 oz) sugar to each 3 dl (½ pint) of liquid. Stir the sugar into the cold juice until completely dissolved. The syrup may be frozen or packed into small, screw-topped, soft drink bottles and sterilized. This syrup may be diluted with hot or cold water (it is excellent to relieve a cold) but is also delicious served undiluted over vanilla ice-cream or meringues.

Recipe from Mary Norwak.

Blackberry and Apple Pie

SERVES SIX-EIGHT
300 g (10 oz) plain flour
125 g (5 oz) butter, cubed
Pinch of salt
Squeeze of lemon juice
8 tablespoons chilled water
2 large cooking apples
450 g (1 lb) blackberries
4 tablespoons sugar

Make the pastry in advance. Sift the flour into a large bowl, add salt and butter and work the fat into the flour with your fingertips until it resembles breadcrumbs. Add the lemon juice and chilled water and quickly mix into a dough. Place in greaseproof paper and put the pastry into the refrigerator for 40 minutes before using. Meanwhile, peel, core and dice the apples and wash the blackberries.

Grease a 25 cm (10 in) pie dish, roll out half of the pastry and cover the base of the dish. Place the blackberries and apple on the pastry and sprinkle sugar over the fruit. Roll out the remaining pastry and cover the pie. If you have any pastry left over, use to decorate the top of the pie. Place in a pre-heated oven, at 190°C (375°F, Mark 5) and bake for 30-35 minutes or until the pastry is golden brown. Serve hot or cold, sprinkled with castor sugar.

This recipe comes from Jacqui Hurst.

Scots Cream Crowdie

SERVES FOUR
6 dl (1 pint) double cream
50 g (2 oz) coarse oatmeal
50 g (2 oz) castor sugar
1 tablespoon rum
100 g (4 oz) fresh blackberries (or raspberries)

Put the oatmeal in a thick-bottomed saucepan and shake it over the heat until crisp. Beat the cream to a thick froth and stir in toasted oatmeal, sugar, rum and fruit. Serve at once. Very rich but scrumptious.

Reproduced by permission of the Hamlyn Publishing Group Ltd from *The Second Country Book* edited by Barbara Hargreaves.

Blackberry Vinegar

1½ kg (3 lb) blackberries
1 kg (2.2 lb) sugar
2 litres (3 pints) malt vinegar

Place blackberries in a bowl and pour vinegar over them. Allow to stand for three days. Stir occasionally. Strain off the liquid, add sugar and boil for ten minutes, then bottle. This is very good for sore throats and makes a delicious piquant sauce.

(Mulberry vinegar can be made in the same way. You can keep the fruit pulp for both blackberry and mulberry vinegar and use it unstrained with batter pudding and suet puddings.)

From Jenny Stone.

Bramble Jelly

1.8 kg (4 lb) blackberries
3 dl (½ pint) water
Juice of 2 lemons
Sugar
¼ teaspoon each of mace, nutmeg and cinnamon (optional)

The jelly sets better if slightly under-ripe berries are used. Wash the fruit and drain well. Put into a preserving pan with the lemon juice and water and simmer for 1 hour until the fruit is soft. Strain through a jelly bag but do not squeeze the pulp or the jelly will be cloudy. Measure the juice and allow 450 g (1 lb) sugar to each 6 dl (1 pint) of juice. Heat the juice gently, stirring in the sugar until dissolved. Boil hard to setting point which will take 10-15 minutes. Pour into hot sterilized jars and cover. If liked, the jelly may be spiced with ¼ teaspoon each of ground mace, nutmeg and cinnamon.

Blackberry and Apple Jam

Makes about 5 kg (10 lb)
2 kg (4 lb) blackberries, washed
3 dl (½ pint) water
750 g (1½ lb) sour cooking apples (peeled, cored and sliced)
3 kg (6 lb) sugar
A knob of butter

Place the blackberries in a large saucepan with half the water and simmer gently until soft. Put the apples in a preserving pan with the remaining water and simmer gently until soft. Pulp with a wooden spoon or a potato masher. Add the blackberries and sugar to the apple pulp, stirring until the sugar has dissolved, then add a knob of butter, bring to the boil and boil rapidly, stirring frequently, for about 10 minutes. Test for a set and when setting point is reached take the pan off the heat and remove any scum with a slotted spoon. Pot and cover the jam in the usual way.

I quote this recipe from *The Good Housekeeping Complete Book of Home Preserving* with permission from the publishers.

Blackberry sorbet and Scots cream crowdie. Photographed September 10.

Blackberry Water Ice

SERVES FOUR
450 g (1 lb) raw blackberries
100 g (4 oz) sugar
1½ dl (¼ pint) water
1 small egg white

Turn the refrigerator to its coldest setting. Make a syrup by boiling the sugar and water for 4 minutes. Allow it to cool. Sieve or mouli the blackberries and mix with syrup. Beat egg white until it forms soft peaks and fold thoroughly into the blackberry mixture. Put into a dish, cover, and freeze to a mush. Stir and freeze for a further half-hour. Stir again and freeze until set, about 2½-3 hours altogether.

This can also be made with wild raspberries.

From *Poor Cook* by Susan Campbell and Caroline Conran, 1971. A super recipe that everyone I know loved.

105

Cooking the dish 'girolles à la forestîere' in the Don Valley near Aberdeen. Photographed August 10.

Chanterelle or **Girolle** *Cantharellus cibarius* Fr. Found in all kinds of woodland but commonly under pines, beeches and birches, they appear from July until the frost of winter puts paid to them. They have a wonderful, egg-yolk yellow colour and if you take a handful you may get a smell similar to fresh apricots. One of the ways of being sure of recognizing them is to make certain that the gills run down the stem.

Chanterelles, or *girolles* as the French call them, are one of the most popular and best known fungi on the Continent and throughout Scandinavia, where they are served in restaurants and sold in shops and markets. The name is derived from the French diminutive of the Greek *kantharos*, a cup.

They keep well for a few days and can also be successfully dried and stored. Chanterelles are superb when cooked with eggs or potatoes and make a succulent filling for an omelette, but my favourite way of serving them is as I have illustrated them à la forestière. Remember, however, when you cook them they tend to give off rather a lot of liquid, especially in wet weather. The excess liquid should be reduced by simmering for 5–10 minutes or, if this is inconvenient, discard it.

Girolles à la Forestière

SERVES FOUR
1½ kg (3 lb) girolles/chanterelles
100 g (4 oz) butter
100 g (4 oz) lean smoked bacon, cut in strips
150 g (6 oz) new potatoes
Parsley, chopped
Salt, black pepper

Wash and trim the mushrooms. Cook them in a bare ounce of butter for 5 minutes, then drain off the liquid. Fry the bacon rapidly in the remaining butter for a few minutes until it begins to brown, then add the girolles and leave to simmer for 20 minutes. Meanwhile, cook the new potatoes and cut them into pieces roughly the size of the mushrooms. Add to the pan of girolles and bacon and stir everything about so that the potatoes colour slightly in the juices – this should take 5 minutes. Season to taste and serve sprinkled with parsley.

This recipe comes from Jane Grigson's excellent book *The Mushroom Feast,* with her permission.

Chanterelles au Gratin

SERVES TWO-FOUR
450 g (1 lb) desirée potatoes
225 g (½ lb) chanterelles
1 clove of garlic, finely chopped
Salt and pepper, butter
3 dl (½ pint) whipping cream
4 tablespoons water
3 tablespoons grated parmesan or cheddar

Grease a casserole with butter and sprinkle with chopped garlic. Peel the potatoes and slice them thinly (I have tried leaving them unpeeled as they are such a pretty colour when young but the thin, stringy bits of skin spoilt the texture). Arrange half the potato slices, overlapping, in the bottom of the dish, season, cover with a layer of chanterelles (I slice the thicker ones), season again and cover with the rest of potatoes. Mix the cream with the water (water helps prevent cream from curdling) and pour over the whole thing. Sprinkle cheese on top, dot with butter and bake for 1½ hours at 180°C (350°F, Mark 4). The top will turn golden brown.

This recipe came to me from Irene Palmer who said that she had adapted it from Jane Grigson's *gratin de pommes de terre aux champignons.* Jane remarks that the affinity between mushrooms and potatoes is remarkable. Irene says, 'It is ambrosial with chanterelles'. I serve this dish with noisettes of lamb or kebabs; they go particularly well together.

Chanterelle Omelette

SERVES TWO
450 g (1 lb) chanterelles
3 shallots, 4 eggs
Butter, salt and black pepper

Caesar's mushrooms ready for cooking in St Arailles, France.
Photographed August 20.

Skin and chop the shallots very finely. Cut away the base of the chanterelle stems, clean and chop them into smallish pieces. Fry them all together in butter for about 5 minutes then pour off the excess liquid, flavour with salt and black pepper, cover to keep hot and put to one side. Meanwhile, prepare a large omelette with 4 eggs, well whipped. When the outside is cooked, but the inside still a bit runny, pour the chanterelles onto one half and flop the other half over the top. Serve piping hot.

Chanterelle Schnapps

Professor Moser from the University of Innsbruck gave me this recipe. He and his students make it in the laboratory.

1 bottle schnapps
10 chanterelles

Dry the chanterelles and then break up into small pieces and add them to the bottle of schnapps; leave for two days and then strain out the fungus. The end result will be a lovely golden yellow liquid with a faint flavour from the chanterelles. Drink very cold.

Caesar's Mushroom *Amanita Caesarea* scop ex Fr. This is a Mediterranean species and has never been found in Britain. I was lucky enough to find this prize collection in an oak wood in southern France. Do not confuse this mushroom with the much redder-coloured fly agaric *Amanita muscaria* which is in Britain!

Caesar's Treat

SERVES FOUR
450 g (1 lb) Caesar's mushrooms
2 cloves of garlic, parsley
Olive oil, butter
Pepper and salt

Cut away the bulbous stem end, clean and chop the mushrooms. Fry them gently in oil and a little butter. After 5 minutes add chopped parsley and finely chopped garlic. Flavour with pepper and salt. Cook rapidly for a further 2 minutes and serve on French packet toast.

Lady's bedstraw. Photographed August 5.

Meadowsweet. My mother's favourite wild flower. Photographed August 1.

Seed heads of poppies. Photographed September 6.

Lady's Bedstraw *Galium verum* L. Lady's bedstraw is a perennial, abundant throughout the British Isles. It is found on grassland, on all but the most acid soils, by roadsides and in hedge-banks and it flowers from July to September.

The most common use of this plant was as a form of rennet to curdle milk when making cheese, giving it the country name of cheese-rennet. In Gloucestershire, it was mixed with nettle juice to make Double Gloucester and in Gerard's time it was used to colour the best Cheshire cheese. According to Ray, the flowering tops, distilled with water, yield an acid liquor which forms a pleasant summer drink.

Meadowsweet *Filipendula ulmaria* L. Maxim. Meadowsweet is common throughout the British Isles. It is found in swamps, marshes, fens, wet woods and meadows, wet rock ledges and by rivers. It is perennial and flowers from June to October.

Meadowsweet, water-mint and vervain were the three herbs held most sacred by the Druids. Often associated with death, it is considered unlucky to bring it into the house. It is said that the scent can induce a deep sleep from which the sleeper may not wake. Meadowsweet was a common strewing herb, used to cover the floors of houses before carpets became known, to impart a pleasant smell to the rooms. John Gerard records this as follows: 'The leaves and floures far excell all other strowing herbes, for to deck up houses, to straw in chambers, halls, and banqueting houses in the summer time; for the smell thereof makes the heart merrie, delighteth the senses: neither doth it cause head-ache, or lothsomenesse to meat, as some othersweet smelling herbs do.'

In medieval times the flowers were used to flavour mead, which, in consequence, it was claimed, became endowed with the taste of the Greek wines. The flowers were also used as a substitute when honey was in short supply because of their very similar flavour. The leaves, too, were used for flavouring wines and preserves and O'Ceirin recommends that it be added to sloe wine 'to impart a wonderful bouquet'.

Heather. Photographed on the Scottish Moors, August 10.

Bell heather. Photographed August 6.

Poppy *Papaver rhoeas* L. The poppy occurs throughout the British Isles and is common in the south but rare elsewhere. The poppy grows as a weed in arable fields and waste places. It is annual or, more rarely, biennial and flowers from June to October.

The poppy is used as an emblem of sleep because of its opium content, and as an emblem of fertility because of the abundance of its seeds. On the Continent the poppy is cultivated for its seeds, which may be used in cakes and confections, but they are mainly grown for the oil which can be expressed from them and which is considered second only to olive oil. In the Middle East the seeds are put to a number of uses: poppy seed cake is a speciality; while in Turkey the peasants mix the seed with olive oil, honey and flour to make tonic cakes; syrup made from the fresh poppy petals is used as an ingredient in soups and gruels, while the foliage is said to have been used as a vegetable.

The seed-heads are ready for picking in September, when they have become grey-brown and have a number of small holes just below the edge of the flat top. If ripe, the seeds can readily be shaken out of these holes. Use the seeds on bread, cakes, pastries, fruit, pasta and other savouries.

Heather *Calluna vulgaris* L. Hull. Heather is an evergreen, common throughout most of the British Isles, excepting an area from the Cotswolds to the Fens. It is found on heaths, moors, bogs and open woods on acid soils. It flowers from July to September.

Heather is named from the heaths on which it is commonly found, while *Calluna* comes from the Greek *kalluna*, to brush, and relates to the use, by country people, of heather stems tightly bound onto a handle to make a broom. An extremely rich blossom on the heather during August and September is reputedly followed by a severe winter, while to burn heather, is said to bring on rain.

Dried heather flowers can be used as a substitute for tea, and 'moorland tea' was a favourite of Robert Burns. Heather shoots have been used instead of hops to flavour beer and a mixture of two parts heather to one part malt was used in the Hebrides. The Celts also prepared an intoxicating decoction of heather and mixed it with wild honey to be drunk at their feasts. A poem, 'Heather Ale', by Robert Louis Stevenson, refers to the Scottish drink but the most legendary recipe of all is that used by the Picts. According to Boethius, they used a secret recipe for preparing a beer or wine from the flowers alone, without the addition of any saccharine matter. Boethius comments that this is quite probable because of the large quantity of honey contained in the heather blossoms, although he suggests the bell heather, *Erica cinerea*, is the most likely ingredient. Legend tells us that in the fourth century the Picts in Shetland were massacred by the Norsemen, leaving only a father and son alive so that they could teach the conquerors the secret of the heather liquor. At first both man and boy refused but, after the torture, the father declared that he would reveal the secret if they first killed his son. Once the boy was dead the father triumphantly declared that, although he had been unsure of his son's powers of endurance, nothing could persuade the father himself to give up the secret, and thus it died with him.

Bell Heather *Erica cinerea* L. Common all over the British Isles, although not in such profusion as ordinary heather, it is the earliest of the two heathers to flower.

Shaggy ink caps. As usual when collecting mushrooms, it was raining. Photographed September 10.

Shaggy Ink Cap *Coprinus comatus* Müll ex Fr. Common in fields, gardens and on roadsides from late in the summer to late autumn. The caps start to turn black and degenerate rather quickly so pick only young caps before the gills have started to blacken. Cook them as soon as you return home.

Shaggy Ink Cap Soup

SERVES FOUR
225 g (8 oz) shaggy ink caps
6 dl (1 pint) chicken stock
Cream
Pepper and salt
Butter
Chopped parsley

Clean the ink caps, discarding the stems, then fry them for 4-5 minutes in butter, remove from the heat and liquidize in an electric blender or pass through a sieve. Return them to the pan and add the chicken stock (home-made is best but it is fine made with a stock cube). Simmer for 15 minutes, flavour with pepper and salt and serve. To each serving add a spoon of cream and a good sprinkling of fresh parsley.

This recipe comes from Yvonne Cocking and is superb. If you find more ink caps than you can eat, they will freeze very well; just fry them in butter and freeze when cooled.

Baked Egg and Ink Caps

SERVES TWO-FOUR
6 ink caps
4 eggs
1 clove garlic
Pepper and salt
Butter

Shaggy ink caps have a very delicate flavour that benefits from a touch of garlic. Clean and chop the ink caps, discarding the stems, and fry for two minutes in butter. Butter four cocotte dishes, add an egg to each and then top with the half-cooked mushrooms. Flavour with pepper and salt and a tiny squeeze of fresh garlic on each. Bake in a pre-heated, hot oven 200°C (400°F, Mark 6). The ink caps reduce a lot on cooking so this sort of dish, where you add them as a flavouring to eggs or something else, is ideal.

Russulas are not a poisonous genus of mushrooms but many of them are quite inedible because of a very hot or bitter flavour. However, many are also edible and some species are especially good. A good test is to taste them in the woods where you find them and to reject any which are at all unpleasant.

The Charcoal Burner *Russula cyanoxantha* Schaeff. ex Secr. Growing as much as 15 cm (6 in) across, it is quite common from summer to late autumn in broad-leaved woods. Probably the best of all the edible russulas, it has a hardish, nutty texture.

*Yellow swamp russula and **Russula nitida** being cooked in a wet birch wood in Scotland. Photographed August 16.*

Yellow Swamp Russula *Russula claroflava* Grove. Up to 7-10 cm (3-4 in) across, it is found in damp birch woods from summer right through to autumn. Geoffrey Kibby, a great mushroom-hunting friend, says that it is his favourite edible mushroom.

Russula nitida Pers, ex Fr. Only up to 6 cm (2-2½ in) across, it can sometimes be found in great profusion in damp birch woods from summer through to autumn. Edible and rather good.

Russula virescens Quel. The green cracked russula is another of the excellent edible russulas found in early autumn in broad-leaved woods.

Russulas on Toast

SERVES TWO-FOUR
450 g (1 lb) russulas
2 shallots
1 clove garlic
50 g (2 oz) butter
4 slices of toast

Clean and trim the russulas without discarding the stems. The washing can be done under a running tap as they don't absorb much water and the leaves and grass stuck to the caps will loosen after they have been run under the tap for a minute or two. Do not peel but chop into 2½ cm (1 in) square pieces. Peel the shallots, slice them rather finely and chop the garlic. Cook for about 2 minutes until they are soft and then add the mushrooms and fry for 8 minutes, stirring occasionally. They are lovely served on toast. Russulas do not break up and go soft like shop mushrooms and they have a slightly crunchy texture with a very mild flavour.

*The charcoal burner **Russula cyanoxantha**. Photographed September 20.*

Goosefoot potage being made with the common spear-leaved orache. Photographed June 16.

On this page I have grouped together the Goosefoot family which provide some of the very best vegetables found in the wild. Members of this family have been eaten for thousands of years and cultivated right up to the present day. The leaves should be picked from the stems and boiled in shallow water as you would spinach.

I have included descriptions of the best-known species and illustrations of some of the most common, but the plants and leaves are very variable and it may prove difficult to differentiate between species. Most species can be found from June right through the summer.

Good King Henry *Chenopodium bonus-henricus* L. A perennial herb, fairly common in most parts of England but rare in Scotland and Ireland, found especially in nitrogen-rich places like pastures, roadsides and farmyards. It flowers from June to September.

The name is said to come from Germany where Henry, or Heinrich, is an elf-name for a woodland creature. Dodoens claims the name was intended to distinguish the plant from a poisonous species called Malus Henricus (Bad Henry). Good King Henry was introduced as a vegetable from central Europe, during Roman times, and was commonly cultivated in medieval and Tudor times. Both this species and fat hen are valuable and versatile food plants, exceptionally rich in vitamin B, iron, calcium and protein. Good King Henry has commonly been used as a pot-herb or boiled like spinach as a green vegetable. The young shoots and flowering tops can be peeled, boiled and dressed like asparagus while the young leaves may be used in salads. The plant can also be made into a soup.

Red Goosefoot *Chenopodium rubrum* L. Common in central and southern England, especially in eastern counties, it can be found in waste places on arable land and as a garden weed. It flowers from July to September.

Fat Hen *Chenopodium album* L. An annual herb very common throughout the British Isles, it occurs in waste places and cultivated land, especially around farmyards. It flowers from June to October.

The generic name for fat hen is taken from the Greek *chen*, a goose, and *pous*, a foot, an allusion to the resemblance of the leaves to the webbed feet of the goose. In Germany the plant is said to have been used for fattening poultry and was known as 'Fette Henne'.

Fat hen has been eaten by man since at least AD 300 having been found in the stomach of the Grauballe Man excavated from the peat bogs of Denmark. It was cultivated as a vegetable all over eastern Europe and in Russia; it is said that during times of scarcity, Napoleon lived on the black bread made from its seeds. It was eaten in the Scottish islands until recent times and in Europe in the last war when the food shortage was acute. The young leaves were eaten as greens or boiled with fat by many tribes of the American Indians, who also ground the seeds into meal to bake as bread, cakes or gruel. Close relatives of *C. album* have been developed into cultivated plants in the American highlands. Two of these crops, quinoa and canahua, are sources of grain, while the third, huauzoutte, is eaten as a vegetable, usually fried in batter.

When picking, gather about three times what you think you are going to need. Use the whole green plant if it is really young, otherwise strip off the side branches and tops to take home, then pull off the leaves and flowers. Cook like spinach. The plant contains iron, calcium and protein and is a valuable addition to the diet.

Common Orache *Atriplex patula* L. Common all over the British Isles except northern Scotland, it flowers from July to September in large clumps on the coast or in wasteland. The most common of the group, with an excellent flavour – very good as a vegetable.

Fat hen. Photographed in a London garden, June 15.

Red goosefoot, often found as a garden weed. Photographed June 18.

Spear-leaved Orache *Atriplex hastata* L. Common in the south and near the sea on shingle beaches above the high-tide mark, flowers from July to September. It is good in soups or as a vegetable.

Goosefoot Potage

SERVES SIX
4 large potatoes
4 cloves garlic
6 heads of shallots or 2 onions
A large bunch of one or more of the goosefoot family
A small bunch of wild sorrel if available
Three tablespoons good olive oil
Salt and black pepper to taste

Peel and cut the potatoes into small pieces and set to boil. Peel and chop the shallots and garlic and fry in the oil in a large pan until soft and slightly browned. By now the potatoes should be boiled and breaking up. Add the potatoes and their water to the shallots and garlic and make up the water to the volume required. Leave to simmer. Now wash the wild vegetables and cut the leaves from the stalks. Chop to fingernail size and add to the pan. Simmer for 20 minutes, flavour and serve. Excellent served the French way with a large crôuton in each bowl. Cut French bread into 1½ cm (½ in) slices and fry in oil with a tiny touch of garlic.

As a Vegetable

Orache, fat hen, Good King Henry or a mixture
Pick the leaves from the stem, wash in cold water and put dripping wet into a pan with an extra spoonful of water to prevent burning. Bring to the boil and cook rapidly for 2 minutes. Drain and press out the water, chop and serve with a knob of butter, fresh ground pepper and salt.

Mugwort *Artemisia vulgaris* L. Common throughout the British Isles but thinning out in northern England and Scotland, it is found in waste places, waysides and hedgerows and flowers from July to September.

In early times it had a reputation as a witch's herb and was used in sorcery and occultism. In the Middle Ages it was used by crystal-gazers as its leaves, 'always turning to the north', were said to be strong in magnetic influence. It was believed to be beneficial to travellers, protecting them from fatigue, sunstroke, wild beasts and evil spirits. It was also effective against consumption, according to the following folk tale:
A charming young girl, whom consumption had brought to the brink of the grave, was lamented by her lover. In a vein of renovating sweetness, a good mermaid sung to him:
Wad ye let the bonnie May die i' your hand,
And the Mugwort flowering i' the land?
He cropped and pressed the flower tops and administered the juice to his fair mistress, who arose and blessed the bestower for the return of health.

On the Continent mugwort was used as an aromatic culinary herb and as a substitute for tea, in the days when the real leaf was expensive. Before the introduction of hops it was also used for flavouring beer and continued to be used in home brewing long after that time. Mugwort may be collected at any time while in bloom and its roots may be dug in the autumn. Although mugwort is well known as an edible herb, I find it has a revolting flavour.

Saffron milk caps being prepared with beans. Photographed in a pine wood in Fife, August 20.

A perfect cauliflower fungus growing at the base of a Scots pine. Photographed September 16.

Saffron Milk Cap *Lactarius deliciosus* L. ex Fr. Found in association with young pines or spruces from July to October but more common in Scotland than in the south, mainly because there are more conifers there. The caps are up to 10 cm (4 in) across. When broken or damaged, *Lactarius* exudes a sort of milky substance. The 'milk' of this species is bright orange and the gills and cap tend to bruise gradually green. This mushroom is much sought after on the Continent; there are many references to eating it in the letters of 19th-century British mushroom hunters.

Lactarius and Beans

SERVES FOUR
150 g (6 oz) haricot beans
1 onion
2 cloves garlic
1 green pepper
450 g (1 lb) salt and pepper
Wild thyme

Soak the beans overnight, then boil gently for two hours until thoroughly soft. Wash mushrooms carefully and chop roughly, stalks included, unless very woody. Chop onion, garlic and half a green pepper, fry in a spoonful of oil or dripping until brown. Add mushrooms and fry – add a little water, or oil if you like your food rich, if necessary. Simmer gently until mushrooms are soft and the liquid is somewhat reduced (milk caps give off a lot of liquid during cooking). Add beans and wild thyme and cook the mixture for another 10-15 minutes. Flavour with pepper and salt. Delicious served with roast lamb.

This recipe comes from Nicky Foy.

Cauliflower or **Brain Fungus** *Sparassis crispa* Wult. ex Fr. Found growing at the base of conifers (especially pine trees) in the autumn, it can grow to as much as 50 cm (20 in) across. Young, fresh specimens are best.

Cauliflower Fungus Treat

SERVES TWO-FOUR
Cauliflower fungus – as much as you have
A little flour
Butter
Salt and pepper
1.5 dl (¼ pint) stock
1 egg yolk
Parsley
A pinch of spice or curry powder

Clean the fungus carefully to remove dirt or insects. Break into large pieces and dust with flour. Fry in butter for 2-3 minutes, then add salt, pepper, chopped parsley and a touch of curry powder. Add the stock. Reduce the liquid by half and then thicken with egg yolk. Serve with a slice of lemon. This fungus is so distinctive and such a delicacy that anyone who has once tried it will be hooked for life.

Beefsteak fungus needs slicing carefuly to make butter-boiled beefsteak. Photographed September 14.

Chicken of the woods growing on a willow in Denham. Photographed July 20.

Chicken of the woods is excellent in a casserole. Photographed September 20.

Beefsteak or **Ox-tongue Fungus** *Fistulina hepatica* Schaeff. ex Fr. Grows on chestnut or oak trees, especially very old oaks, usually close to the ground and found in the late summer or autumn. Make sure you have fresh specimens that have not gone woody. The fungus will tend to exude a reddish juice which helps to make the sauce delicious when it is cooked. The fungus is highly thought of as an esculent on the Continent but in Britain it is little used – mistakenly, I think.

Butter-boiled Beefsteak

450 g (1 lb) beefsteak fungus
6 shallots
3 cloves garlic
Thyme
Pepper and salt
Butter

Clean and cut the beefsteak fungus into fine slices and place in a frying pan with finely chopped shallots and garlic. Barely cover with water and simmer for 10 minutes. Add pepper, salt, thyme and a generous knob of butter and cook until the liquid has reduced to a thick sauce. This is a really 5-star dish; definitely one of my favourite mushroom recipes.

Chicken of the Woods or **Sulphur Polypore** *Laetiporus sulphureus* Bull ex Fr. Well known in German-speaking countries, it is usually parboiled and fried in oil or bacon fat. It is also much sought after in the USA where it is used as a valuable addition to casseroles. It grows on old trees, usually yew, oak, sweet chestnut or willow, at any time of year except winter. Like other tree-growing fungi it becomes tough and bitter with age so only fresh, young specimens should be collected. You can tell if it is too old by the colours, which tend to fade from striking bright yellows and oranges to dull yellow and, finally, pure white.

Chicken of the Woods Casserole

This recipe was given to me by Geoffrey Kibby, who was served it by friends in the USA. If you have found a really good collection you may easily have 2 kg (4 lb) of fresh fungus. Any not needed for immediate use can be kept in the fridge for a few days or deep frozen, having been chopped up and lightly fried in butter.

Take about 250-500 g, (10-20 oz) of the fungus (cut away old or damaged parts) and clean away any dirt with a damp cloth. Cut into neat cubes about 1½ cm (½ in) square and add them to any casserole dish a good half-hour before serving. I think they are particularly good with pork and beef. If not cooked for too long the cubes will retain their shape and colour and add a delicious taste and texture to the casserole.

Photographed at Denham, on the canal bank, September 15.

Elder *Sambucus nigra* L. Elderberries gathered on St John's Eve were traditionally thought to protect the possessor against witchcraft and also to bestow magical powers. In Hertfordshire, traditional fare at the feast of St Catherine (kept until the latter part of the 19th century) included 'Kattern' or 'Kat' cakes eaten hot and buttered with hot elderberry wine. The Romans used the juice of the berries as a hair dye and there is a tradition of using the dried berries as a substitute for raisins (in such things as 'barm brack' or 'curney cake'). The cordial has long been used for colds and coughs and has recently been proved to be scientifically effective. Elderberries contain viburnic acid which induces perspiration and is especially useful in cases of bronchitis and similar troubles.

Elderberry wine has always had a good reputation and was once so popular that whole orchards of elders were planted in Kent and the berries sold for wine-making. Elderberries have also been used in the manufacture of British wines and in the adulteration of foreign wines. For example, certain 'clarets' and 'Bordeaux' were actually based on elderberry wine flavoured with small amounts of vinegar, sugar and port wine. Cheap port was also doctored with elderberry juice to improve the flavour and colour, to the extent that in the middle of the 18th century the cultivation of elder trees was forbidden in Portugal.

In 1899 an American sailor informed a physician of Prague that getting drunk on genuine, old, dark-red port was a sure remedy for rheumatic pains. This observation started a long series of investigations ending in the discovery that genuine port wine has practically no anti-neuralgic properties. But the cheap stuff, faked to resemble tawny port by the addition of elderberry juice, often banishes the pain of sciatica and other forms of neuralgia, though it is of no avail in genuine neuritis. The dose recommended is 30 g (1 oz) elderberry juice mixed with 10 grams (¼-½ oz) of port wine. Elderberries also make good pies if blended with spices and used,

Elderberries can be found in such profusion it is a crime not to put them to some use. Here they are shown made into wine, elderberry syrup, and with the ingredients for elderberry and apple jelly.

formerly, to be preserved with spices and kept for winter use when fruit was scarce.

Light Elderberry Wine

450 g (1 lb) elderberries
Pectin enzyme
Wine yeast
2 campden tablets
1 kg (2.2 lb) sugar

Pull the berries off the stalks with a dinner fork and crush them thoroughly in a strong polythene bag with a rolling pin, or similar implement, to break the skins. Add 1.2 litres (2 pints) boiling water and campden tablets and leave overnight in a covered container. Next day, add 2½ litres (4 pints) warm water, pectin and activated wine yeast. Put in a gallon jar and fit airlock; leave for 3 days. Colour will return to normal at this stage. Strain through jelly bag and return to clean jar. Insert airlock and leave in a warm place (75-80° F) to ferment out (approximately 6 weeks). Syphon off sediment into clean jar and leave to clear. Repeat this process if necessary. Bottle and store in a cool place.

This wine can be made in September and 'mulled' for Christmas with great success or it can be kept for a few more months to provide a splendid, dry table wine. It does not improve after two years of keeping.

This recipe is from Jill Ingham of South Woodchester. This rather small quantity of fruit makes a very palatable light wine. If, however, you would prefer a stronger, slightly sweeter, wine, increase the elderberries to 900 g (2 lb) and the sugar to 1½ kg (3¼ lb). A stronger wine like this one will improve after keeping for a year or two.

119

Red-berried elder. Photographed in Scotland, August 15.

Red-berried Elder *Sambucus racemosa* L. Rather frequent in Scotland but rare elsewhere, it was introduced as a garden shrub from Europe but has now become naturalised. It fruits rather earlier than the native elder, ripening in August. It can be used in the ordinary elderberry recipes with, or in place of, the dark berries.

Elderberry and Apply Jelly

1.3 kg (3 lb) cooking apples
2.2 litres (4 pints) elderberries
1.2 litres (2 pints) water
Sugar
Peel of an orange and ½ stick cinnamon tied together with cotton

Wash apples well. Cut them up and put in a pan with the elderberries. Add the water, cover the pan and simmer to a pulp. Turn into a jelly bag and drip overnight. Measure juice and allow 450 g (1 lb) sugar to 6 dl (1 pint) of juice. Put juice and sugar into a large pan and heat gently until sugar has dissolved, then add orange rind and cinnamon. Boil rapidly until setting point is reached. Remove orange and cinnamon. Pour into small, warmed jam jars and seal. This is a soft jelly.

Quoted from *A Fenland Village Cookery Book* by Liz Roman.

Elderberry Syrup

Ripe elderberries
Sugar

Pick the fruit on a dry day. Wash well and drain thoroughly. Strip the fruit from the stems and put into a pan, adding just enough water to cover. Simmer for 30 minutes until the berries are very soft. Strain through a jelly bag or muslin and measure the juice. Allow 450 g (1 lb) sugar and 10 cloves to each 6 dl (1 pint) of juice. Heat the juice gently, stirring in the sugar until dissolved. Boil for 10 minutes and then leave until cold. The syrup may be frozen in small quantities or packed into small, screw-topped, soft drink bottles which have been sterilized.

Elderberry syrups of this kind have been used since Tudor times as a stand-by against winter colds. The syrup is a cold aperient, relieves all chest troubles, will stop a cold and bring on a sweat. It is normally diluted, allowing 2 tablespoons of syrup to a tumbler of hot water and a squeeze of lemon juice. A little whisky may be added if liked. A few drops added to a glass of wine makes an excellent apéritif.

This recipe comes from Mary Norwak.

Guelder rose berries. Photographed September 25.

Elderberry Pickle

675 g (1½ lb) elderberries (weighed off stems)
50 g (2 oz) light, soft brown sugar
12 g (½ oz) ground ginger
¼ teaspoon ground black pepper
Pinch ground cloves
1 medium onion
3 dl (½ pint) cider vinegar
1 teaspoon salt
Pinch ground mace
50 g (2 oz) seedless raisins

Wash the elderberries very well and drain thoroughly. Sieve the berries, pressing out all the juice, to make a thin purée. Put into a pan with the finely chopped onion and all the other ingredients. Bring to the boil and then simmer, stirring well, for 20 minutes. Put into small, sterilized jars and cover with vinegar-proof lids.

Guelder Rose *Viburnum opulus* L. A large, deciduous shrub or small tree, generally rather common (but less so in Scotland), it is found in woods, scrub and hedges, especially on damp soils. The guelder rose flowers from June to July and bears fruit in September and October.

The name guelder comes from Gueldersland, a Dutch province, where the tree was first cultivated. The berries have been used in different ways by different nations. In Norway and Sweden they were used to flavour a paste of honey and flour. In Siberia they were fermented with flour and then distilled to yield a spirit. In Canada they are widely used as a substitute for cranberries and also to make a piquant jelly and in Maine, in the United States, they are cooked with molasses.

Juniper tree in the Lake District. Photographed April 16.

Juniper berries. Photographed on the Chiltern Hills, September 20.

Guelder Rose Jelly

MAKES 1 kg (2 lb)
450 g (1 lb) fresh guelder berries
Rind of one orange
3 dl (½ pint) water
450 g (1 lb) granulated sugar

Pick over the guelder berries and discard any bruised or rotten
ones. Place in a saucepan and add the finely grated orange rind and
the water. Bring to the boil over a moderate heat and simmer for 10
minutes. Stir occasionally with a wooden spoon. The guelder
berries will pop and the mixture will become a thick pulp. Take the
pan off the heat and press the berries and liquid through a sieve to
make a purée. Return the purée to the saucepan and add the sugar.
Stir over a low heat until the sugar has dissolved and then bring to
the boil. As soon as the first small bubbles appear around the edge
of the pan, draw off the heat. Pour into clean, warm jars and leave
to set. Cover and seal when cold.

Juniper *Juniperus communis*. L. The juniper is a small, evergreen
tree or shrub, locally common in the south and south-east of
England, the Lake District and the far north. In Ireland it is
common on the west and north-west coasts. The juniper grows on
chalk downs, heaths, moors and pine and birch woods and it is
often dominant in scrub on chalk, limestone and slate. It flowers in
May and June and the berries ripen in September and October.

Juniper was used as a protective charm in earlier days. Its
branches were hung above doors and windows on May Eve to keep
away witches and it was burnt during outbreaks of the plague and
sweating sickness. The smoke from a juniper fire was said to keep
demons away, while infusions of the berries would restore lost
youth. To dream of a juniper tree was considered unlucky,
although to dream of the berries was often a good omen, foretelling

coming success or the birth of an heir. Juniper berries are used to
produce the volatile oil which is a prime ingredient of gin. The oil is
the source of the flavour and diuretic properties of the spirit.

The berries have also been used for many other purposes. They
can be roasted and ground as a coffee substitute or infused as a
herb tea, as practised in Lapland. On the Continent there used to
be considerable demand for 'Roob' or 'Rob of Juniper', an aqueous
extract of the berries. The berries are crushed, macerated with
water, distilled and the residue evaporated to a soft consistency.
The distilled oil is, in this case, a by-product. In Sweden, the
berries are used to make a health beer and a conserve; the beer-like
'genevrette' is made in France by fermenting equal parts of juniper
berries and barley. In Germany, the berries are used as a culinary
spice, particularly to flavour sauerkraut and in England, they have
been used as a substitute for pepper.

The berries make an excellent survival food because they are
available through the winter. Some American Indian tribes
preserve them by drying, then grind them and bake them into
cakes. These Indians also eat the inner bark in times of hardship
and boil the stems and leaves to make an astringent tea. The berries
are green in their first year and are not ripe until they turn black, in
their second year on the bush. It is at this stage that they are rich in
the oil which is the source of their value as a flavouring.

121

Parasol mushrooms being made into parasol fritters and mushroom and potato pan scones. Photographed September 25.

Shaggy parasols. Photographed in a London square, August 18.

Parasol Mushroom *Lepiota procera* Scop, ex Fr. Fairly common in pastures and open woods. As they normally stand well above the grass, they are easily spotted from as early as July until as late as November, if there are no bad frosts. For the best combination of size and tenderness, pick just when the cap begins to open. A single mushroom should be enough for one person. The flesh is very delicate and is best cooked rather quickly. Apart from the recipes I have quoted below, they are also excellent in a flan with bacon.

Parasol Fritters

SERVES TWO
Batter
4 large parasols
50 g (2 oz) plain flour
1 egg
1½ dl (¼ pint) milk
Pinch of salt
½ teaspoon mixed herbs
Black pepper
2 teaspoons melted butter
Light oil

Beat egg, milk and butter together with seasoning until smooth. Wash parasols, remove stems, cut into quarters and coat lightly in flour. Dip in batter and deep fry until golden brown. Drain on absorbent paper. Serve hot with courgettes or broccoli for a main course, or on their own as a starter. The mushrooms are unbelievably succulent served like this.

Mushroom and Potato Pan Scones

SERVES TWO
75 g (3 oz) grated cheese
100 g (4 oz) cooked potatoes
225 g (8 oz) sliced mushroom (blewits, parasols and chopped
*   puff-ball can all be used)*
25 g (1 oz) butter
Seasoning – pepper, salt, mixed herbs
100 g (4 oz) self-raising flour
Milk to mix.

Mash potatoes (do not add milk) with seasoning. Sieve flour and rub in butter. Chop mushrooms into small pieces. Add potatoes, cheese and mushrooms to flour. Mix to a firm consistency with a little milk and form into balls. Lightly grease pan, pat scones into 5 cm (2 in) wide by 12 mm (½ in) deep circles and cook steadily on each side for 3 minutes or until golden brown.

Serve as a snack or with salad.

Both these recipes come from S.L. Shute at the Natural History Museum.

Shaggy Parasol *Lepiota rhacodes* var. *hortensis* Pilat. Rather smaller and shorter-stemmed than the ordinary parasol mushroom and when cut or damaged, the flesh quickly turns pink. It is usually found in gardens, often on rubbish heaps, from summer to autumn. There are two varieties of shaggy parasol, the other, *Lepiota rhacodes* (Vitt.) Quel., is usually found in woods or shrubberies. Both are excellent to eat and can be cooked in the same way as parasol mushrooms, or else rapidly fried in butter with onion.

Rowan wine beginning to ferment. Photographed on Snake Pass, Derbyshire, October 1.

Rowan or **Mountain Ash** *Sorbus aucuparia* (L.) Ehrh. A small deciduous tree, common throughout the British Isles, it is found in woods, scrub and on mountains. The mountain ash flowers in May and June and bears fruit from August to November. The berries may hang on the tree until January but they are best picked in October when they have their full colour but have not yet become mushy. Cut the clusters whole from the trees and trim off any excess stalk.

The mountain ash has many connections with tradition and superstition, particularly relating to witches. On May Eve rowan crosses were worn and were fastened to cattle to give protection against witchcraft. The crosses had to be made without the use of a knife. Branches of rowan were brought indoors on Good Friday for the same purpose. Red thread was traditionally used in conjunction with the rowan:

> *Rowan tree and red thread*
> *Make the witches tine their speed.*
> *[to tine = to lose]*

The following story was told to the Rev. George Ormsby by an

Rowan jelly. A traditional Scottish recipe. Photographed October 4.

old man who used to work in the vicarage garden. The tailor of the neighbouring village had applied to the old man for two small branches from a mountain ash which grew in his garden. On being asked why they were wanted, the applicant stated that his wife had been churning for hours and yet no butter would come; thus, they believed the cream was bewitched. They had heard say, that if the cream was stirred with one twig of mountain ash and the cow beaten with the other, the charm would be broken and the butter would come without delay.

The Celtic people fermented the fruit into wine and the Scots, in particular, distilled it to a powerful spirit. The ancient Irish used it to flavour alcoholic drinks, especially mead, while the Welsh used to brew an ale from the berries and a wholesome perry or cider can also be made from them. In recent times, its most common use has been as a tart, but agreeable, jelly that is the traditional accompaniment to venison and is also excellent with cold game or fowl. The juice of freshly squeezed rowan berries can be added to gin in place of angostura bitters.

Rowan Wine

A DRY WINE – MAKES ONE GALLON
1 kg (2.2 lb) rowan berries
2 oranges
2 litres (½ gallon) boiling water
1.3 kg (3 lb) sugar
2 teaspoons dried yeast

Pick the berries when ripe and remove all the stalks. Wash carefully and put into a white or uncoloured plastic bucket. (They smell awful at this stage.) Leave the must for 3 days, stirring daily, then strain through a muslin bag into a gallon jar. Make up the sugar syrup with 1.3 kg (3 lb) sugar and 9 dl (1½ pints) water. Pour into the jar, grate the orange rind and squeeze juice into the jar. Start yeast fermenting, then add to the wine. Put a cotton wool bung into the neck of the jar and leave for 3 days. Then put on airlock and leave to ferment for about 4 months. This wine clears quickly. Syphon into a clean jar and leave for at least 6 months. It is a long time before this wine becomes drinkable so leave it as long as you can. From Jenny Stone.

Rowan Jelly

1.3 kg (3 lb) rowans
900 g (2 lb) juicy apples, pale, soft brown sugar

Peel, slice and core apples. Place in 12 dl (2 pints) of water and boil for 20 minutes until soft. Add the rowans and simmer to a pulp. Strain through a jelly bag. Add 450 g (1 lb) sugar to each 6 dl (1 pint) of juice. First warm the sugar, boil the juice for 10 minutes and then add the sugar. Boil for another 10 minutes, skimming all the time. Pour into jars and tie down at once.

From Lyndsay Shearer, out of May Buchan's *Common Place Book*. This is a lovely old recipe but I found the brown sugar tends to make too strong a taste so I prefer to use white. The addition of apples is fine from a taste point of view but should be deleted if you want a clear jelly.

Whitebeam *Sorbus aria* (L.) Crantz. A deciduous tree or shrub native from Kent and Hertfordshire to Dorset and the Wye Valley, found in woods and scrub, usually on chalk or limestone. The whitebeam flowers in May and June and bears fruit in September. The bunched red berries are edible as soon as they begin to 'blet' or go rotten, like medlars.

Giant puff-ball, an excellent addition to a cooked breakfast. Photographed October 13.

Ordinary puff-balls. This species is **Lycoperdon perlatum.** *Photographed October 5.*

The miller. Collected in the New Forest. September 29.

Giant Puff-ball *Langermannia gigantea* (Batsch ex Pers.) Rostk. Uncommon, but so remarkable for its size that it has the reputation of being more common than it is. It can grow almost anywhere but is usually found in pastures, near hedges, in summer and autumn.

The word 'puff-ball' is a corruption of Puck or Poukball, anciently called Puck-fish. The Irish name is Pooks-foot from the Saxon, 'Pulker-fish', a toadstool. The American Indians used various species of puff-balls, eaten in their early stages of growth, either raw, boiled or roasted. The Zunis dried them for winter use, while the Iroquois fried them and added them to soups. The Omaga Indians cut the giant puff-ball into chunks and fried it like meat. When picked for consumption the flesh should still be pure white. As they age, the flesh turns yellowish. A good, young specimen can be kept in the fridge for a few days.

Crunchy Puff-ball

SERVES FOUR
Young puff-ball
6 slices bacon
1 egg
50 g (2 oz) flour
Fresh breadcrumbs, toasted
Salt and pepper

Make fresh breadcrumbs and toast them under the grill. Make a batter by whipping the egg lightly with a little water, then gradually mix in the flour. Flavour with pepper and salt and leave for 20 minutes for the flour to swell. Clean the puff-ball (it is usually unnecessary to peel it), then cut into slices about ½ cm (¼ in) thick. Dip first in the batter and then in the breadcrumbs and fry in the fat created by frying the bacon, until they are a lovely, golden brown. Serve with bacon, for breakfast.

This is a very traditional recipe, enhanced by Jacqui Hurst's idea of the toasted breadcrumbs.

Savoury Puff-ball

SERVES THREE-FOUR
1 medium puff-ball
450 g (1 lb) beef, finely cubed
1 large onion
3 medium courgettes
3-6 dl (½-1 pint) stock made from ½ teaspoon
mixed herbs, 1 stock cube, 1 teaspoon tomato purée, salt and pepper

Lightly fry onions to a golden brown in a little fat. Add beef, mix well, season and fry until cooked, turning frequently. Drain excess fat, slice courgettes and lightly fry (fat drained from meat may be used). Slice the puff-ball and layer in a deep casserole with meat, onion and courgettes. Add stock. Cover dish with foil or lid and bake at 190°C (375°F, Mark 5) for 1½-2 hours (may be slow-baked for longer). Serve with baked potatoes.

This recipe has been slightly adapted from one I received from Sharon Shute.

There are many species of puff-ball that are good to eat and none in Britain that are poisonous. The earth-balls on the other hand are not edible. Always make sure that any puff-ball you are collecting to eat is young and fresh. They must be white right through, so if they are beginning to yellow, discard them.

Cook and use all species of puff-ball as you would the giant puff-ball or you can cut them in thin slices, dry them and then fry them some time later without first soaking them in water. The result is a puff-ball (potato) crisp!

Among the best species to eat are:

Lycoperdon perlatum Pers. Found in woodlands, it grows to about 8 cm (3 in) height.

Lycoperdon pyriforme Schaeff. ex Pers. Found in large clumps, it grows on rotten stumps or on the ground near stumps, to a height of about 4 cm (1½-2 in).

Calvatia utriformis (Bull ex Pers.) Jaap. Found in pastures or on heaths, it is more common in the north. This is the largest puff-ball after the giant puff-ball and often may be as much as 15 cm (6 in) high.

Bovista plumbea Pers. ex Pers. Found on short grass on lawns, pastures and such places as golf courses, it grows to about 3 cm (1 in) across. This type of puff-ball is only very delicately attached to the ground and so is often seen rolling around unattached.

Vascellum pratense (Pers.) Kreisel. Found in pastures and on lawns and golf courses, it is usually yellowish in colour on the outside but this does not mean that the inside has gone too far to eat. Its size is about 3 cm (1 in) across.

Gale being gathered. There is enough in the jar to make about 12 litres (3 gallons). Photographed September 29.

Bog Myrtle *Myrica gale* L. A small, strongly aromatic shrub occurring throughout the British Isles in bogs and on wet heaths and fens. It flowers in April and May and the fruits are borne in August and September. It is also known as sweet gale.

Bog myrtle leaves were used for flavouring ale long before hops were brought to England and in Sweden it was forbidden to gather the blossoms before a certain date, in order to preserve the plant. In many places the berries were dried and used as a spice for flavouring soups and stews. The French, in Canada, used the leaves

for a similar purpose, while in the Highlands they were dried and used to scent linen and keep moths away. The Swedes put a sprig of gale in neat spirit (fire-water) and leave it for a month or two. They then serve it with the roe of bleak as a special delicacy.

Gale Mead

1 handful fresh gale leaves
4½ litres (1 gallon) water
450 g (1 lb) honey, 1 lemon, yeast

Hops can be found wild on hedges, especially in central and southern England. Photographed September 30.

Boil the water and then pour it on to the gale leaves. Add the honey and the juice of the lemon and stir well to melt all the honey. Activate the yeast. When the water has cooled down to blood heat, add the yeast and leave in the open bucket to ferment for 4-5 days. Strain off and bottle in screw-top bottles. The mead will be ready to drink in a week. After bottling, keep testing the bottles to see that they don't get too fizzy; my first bottles ended up all over the ceiling! If they do not fizz at all, add a teaspoonful of sugar to each one and leave for a week.

Hop *Humulus lupulus* L. Although hops for brewing beer were not introduced in England until the 16th century, they had been used on the Continent from the earliest times. There is a reference to the use of hops in beer-making in the Finnish saga *Kalevala*, thought to date back some 3000 years. The planting of hops was forbidden in the reign of Henry VI but, in the 16th century, Flemish settlers began cultivating hops in Kent and this is still the most important hop-growing county in Britain. The impossibility of distinguishing between cultivated plants and wild plants suggests that little, if any, improvement of the indigeneous hop was achieved during the primary domestication.

When hops were first imported into England in about 1520, the more bitter drink produced was rejected by many people and was even banned by Henry VIII, who loved spiced ale and 'interfered in everything from religion to beer barrels'. Before hops were introduced, the traditional drink in England, in both town and country, was ale which was brewed from malt and yeast only, or from malt, yeast and honey flavoured with heath tops, ground ivy, marjoram, yarrow, broom or any other bitter or aromatic herbs. Andrew Boorde in his *Dyetary of Health* says, 'Ale is made of malte and water; and they the which do put any other thynge to ale than is rehersed, except yeast, barme or godesgood do sophysticat theyr ale. Ale for an Englyshe man is a naturall drynke. Ale must have these properties; it must be fresshe and cleare, it must not be ropy nor smoky, nor it must have no weft nor tayle. Ale should not be dronke under .v. days olde . . . Berre is made of malte, of hoppes, and water; it is a naturall drynke for a Dutche man. And now of late dayes it is moche used in England to the detryment of many Englysshee men.'

The union of hops and malt is amusingly described in one of the Brasenose College ale poems:

A Grand Cross of Malta, one night at a ball,
Fell in love with and married 'Hoppetta the Tall'.
Hoppetta, the bitterest, best of her sex,
By whom he had issue – the first, 'Double X'.

Three others were born by this marriage – a girl,
Transparent as Amber and precious as Pearl.
Then a son, twice as strong as a Porter or Scout,
And another as 'spruce' as his brother was 'Stout'.

Double X, like his Sister, is brilliant and clear,
Like his Mother, tho' bitter, by no means severe:
Like his Father, not small, and resembling each brother,
Joins the spirit of one to the strength of the other.

(From 'Aarne', 1961)

Carter, 1749, says that hops are chosen 'by their bright green colour, sweet smell, and clamminess, when rubb'd between the hands'. It is the ripened cones of the female plant that are used in brewing, therefore only female plants are cultivated. The principal activity of hops is in the glandular hairs of the cone which contains lupulin, a sedative and hypnotic drug.

Beer

½ litre (1 pint) hops
225 g (8 oz) malt
225 g (8 oz) sugar
Yeast
4½ litres (1 gallon) water

Boil the hops for 15 minutes, then strain off the liquid into a bucket. Mix in the sugar and the malt. Activate the yeast and when the liquor has cooled down, add the yeast. Leave in the covered bucket for 5 days then bottle in screw-top bottles, leaving the sediment behind. Test the bottles occasionally to see that they do not get too fizzy. If, however, they are flat, add a teaspoon of sugar to each bottle and leave for a week. The beer can normally be drunk 10 days to 2 weeks after you start making it. Pour it carefully into a jug, leaving any sediment behind.

Crab Apple Cheese with its sharp flavour offsets the fattiness of Pork. Photographed September 25.

Crab Apple *Malus sylvestris* Mill. The crab apple is common throughout England, Wales, Ireland and the Channel Isles. It occurs north to Ross but is rare in central and north Scotland. It may be found in woods, hedges and scrub. It is deciduous and flowers in May. The apples can be picked from August to November but are normally at their best at the end of September or early October.

There are two subspecies of crab apples in Britain: *sylvestris,* the real native crab which is a little, round apple ending up a pure yellow colour when ripe; and *mitis,* which is normally larger and more apple-shaped than round; this one, it would seem, has descended from cultivated apples reverting to a wild form.

Apples of all sorts have been eaten by man since the dawn of time. The charred remains of small apples were found in the prehistoric Swiss lake dwellings and there are references to apples in all the early books of food and medicine. The Ancient Britons cherished the apple, both for food and beverage purposes. Crab apples are the origin of all cultivated varieties and are still used as a rootstock. Because the apple is such an ancient and valued fruit there are many traditions and customs connected with it.

It has always been a symbol of fruitfulness and plenty and, of all fruit trees, apples were considered the most magic. To sleep under an apple tree rendered one liable to be carried off by the fairies. A single spray of apple blossom flowering among ripe apples portends the death of one of the family, while the oldest tree in an orchard contains the Apple Tree Man, responsible for the fruitfulness of the orchard, who was customarily left the last apple of each year's crop. Witches often worked ill by the gift of an apple and used the skins in divination.

Apples were also used in experiments for love and favour. For example, every person present in a room fastens a length of string to an apple and suspends it before the fire. The apples are considered to fall in an order corresponding to the order in which the owners will be married. The owner of the last apple to fall will remain single. To test the fidelity of your lover, place an apple pip in the fire, saying his name as you do so. If the lover is faithful the pip will make a noise as it bursts with the heat, but if he is not, the pip will burn away silently. Devon girls gathered crab apples from the hedge and arranged them in the shape of their suitors' initials. At dawn on Michaelmas Day they would steal down and look at them. The initials in the best condition were those of the future husband. If you eat an apple at midnight upon Allhallows Eve without looking behind you and then gaze into a mirror, you will see the face of your future husband or wife.

The crab apple has also been the subject of several proverbs and expressions. The sourness of it gives rise to the expression 'a crab' or 'crabby', meaning an ill-tempered person (sour as a crab apple). Other characteristics of the tree are described in the following verse:

> *The crab of the wood*
> *Is sauce very good*
> *For the crab of the sea;*
> *But the wood of the crab*
> *Is sauce for crab*
> *That will not her husband obey.*

It is said that the older the crab-tree, the more crabs it bears. Verjuice is a fermented brew made from either crab apples or sour grapes. It keeps in the bottle, like wine, and was used by medieval cooks in many dishes, as we would use lemon juice. Crab apples have long been used in drinks. 4000 years ago cider made from crab apples and mead from wild honey were probably the common drinks of our ancestors. Another ancient drink is the Wassail Bowl. The chief ingredients were strong ale, sugar, spices and roasted crabs. Traditionally people kept wassail on Twelfth Night and Christmas Eve, as in *Hamlet*:

> *The King doth wake tonight, and takes his rouse,*
> *Keeps wassail, and the swaggering upspring reels.*

Puck, in *A Midsummer Night's Dream,* put the crabs to good use:

> *And sometimes lurk I in a gossip's bowl,*
> *In very likeness of a roasted crab,*
> *And when she drinks against her lips I bob,*
> *And on her withered dewlap pour the ale.*

Verjuice

Gather some ripe crab apples and lay them in a heap to sweat, then throw away the stalks and decayed fruit and, having mashed the apples, express the juice. A cider or wine press will be useful for this purpose. Strain it and in a month it will be ready, It is the best, simple substitute for lemon juice that can be found and answers still better in place of sorrel. The French, for many dishes, prefer verjuice to lemon.

Crab Apple Jelly

Crab apples make a beautiful pink jelly with a lovely flavour – great on scones or toast for tea.

2 kg (4 lb) crab apples
1-1½ litres (2 pints) water
Granulated or preserving sugar

Wash and cut up (or chop) the crab apples. Place in a preserving pan with water just to cover – about 1.2 litres (2 pints). Bring slowly to the boil, then simmer the fruit gently for about 1 hour. Stir occasionally and mash the crab apples once or twice with a potato masher to really break up the fruit and extract the pectin.

Ladle the softened fruit and juice into a scalded jelly bag and allow juice to drip for several hours. Measure the strained juice back into the rinsed preserving pan and for each 5 dl (1 pint) of juice add 450 g (1 lb) sugar. Stir over a low heat until sugar has dissolved and then bring to the boil. Boil rapidly until setting point is reached – about 10-15 minutes. When ready, drain off the heat and skim, then pot quickly in small heated jars. Crab apple jelly sets very fast. This recipe comes from Katie Stewart.

Crab Apple Wine

MEDIUM SWEET – MAKES ONE GALLON
1 kg (2 lb) crab apples
1 orange
1.2 kg (3 lb) sugar
2 litres (½ gallon) boiling water
225 g (8 oz) cooking apples
1 lemon, yeast

Pick crab apples when really ripe and mix with cooking apples. Grate all the apples into a plastic bucket, using only a stainless-steel grater, or crush them well. Pour on boiling water, allow to cool, then mash with hand. Allow wine must to stand for three days. Stir daily. Now strain through wine bag into a gallon jar. Make up sugar syrup with 8 dl (1½ pints) of water and 1.2 kg (3 lb) of sugar and pour into wine jar. Grate orange and lemon rind and squeeze juice into jar. Prepare yeast and allow to ferment for a while, then put into wine jar and make up liquid with boiled, cooled water to correct amount. Leave wine to ferment for four months, then syphon into a clean gallon jar and leave for further three months. Another good wine can be made with 1 kg (2 lb) of crab apples and 450 g (1 lb) of blackberries using the same method as above.

Recipe from Jenny Stone.

Crab Apple Cheese

1½ kg (3 lb) crab apples
3 dl (½ pint) sweet cider
½ teaspoon ground cinnamon
Granulated or light, soft brown sugar
3 dl (½ pint) water
½ teaspoon ground cloves
½ teaspoon ground nutmeg

Wash the apples and drain them well. Cut them into pieces without peeling or coring and put into a pan with the water and cider and simmer until the fruit is very soft. Press through a sieve and weigh the purée. Allow 450 g (1 lb) sugar to each 450 g (1 lb) of purée. Stir in the sugar over low heat until it has dissolved completely. Add the spices and bring to the boil. Reduce heat to simmering and simmer until thick, stirring well. Pour into sterilized jars with straight sides and cover. This is excellent for a sweet course but is also delicious served with pork, ham, duck or goose.

A lovely recipe from Mary Norwak.

Sloes growing in France. Photographed August 30.

Bullace or wild greengage growing in Suffolk. Photographed September 26.

Sloe or **Blackthorn** *Prunus spinosa* L. A deciduous shrub common from Sutherland southwards and throughout Ireland, it occurs in scrub, woods and hedges on a great variety of soils. It flowers from March to May and bears fruit in September and October. The best time to pick the sloes is after the first frost as this makes the skins softer and more permeable.

The sloe is the ancestor of our cultivated plums. Man has been eating it for thousands of years. The sloe makes such a good wine that, according to Brook, 200 years ago it was much used 'by fraudulent wine merchants in adulterating port wine, for which purpose it is well adapted on account of its astringency, slight acidity, and deep red colour. It has been stated that there is more port wine (so called) drank in England alone, than is manufactured in Portugal'. Researches at Holy Cross Abbey in Ireland showed that the medieval monks were partial to sloes in the form of an alcoholic drink akin to gin. The leaves have also been made into a rather astringent tea (Irish tea). The flowering of the blackthorn is often accompanied by a cold spell, and this is known as 'blackthorn winter'.

Bullace *Prunus domestica* subspecies *insititia* L. C.K. Schneid. Found growing wild in hedges near orchards and gardens from which it presumably escaped years ago, the fruit is blue-black and larger than sloes. The damson is usually thought to be a cultivated form of bullace.

Prunus domestica subspecies *italica* (Borkh.) Hegi. Very closely related to the previous subspecies it is, in fact, also known as bullace. This is presumed to be an escape from cultivation and is found in hedges. The fruit is green like the domestic greengage.

Sloe Gin

Sloes, pricked with a fork
50 g (2 oz) barley sugar or almond essence
1 bottle gin

Half fill two clean, dry, wine bottles with the pricked fruit. Add to each 25 g (1 oz) crushed barley sugar or 2-3 drops of almond essence. Fill the bottles with gin. Cork securely and allow to remain in a moderately warm place for 3 months. Strain the liquor through fine muslin or filter paper until quite clear. Bottle, cork securely and store for use.

Adapted from Mrs Beeton's *Book of Household Management*.

The resultant liquor is so strong that I advise melting the barley sugar in a little water which will slightly weaken the end product and also ensure that you get 2 full bottles from 1 bottle of gin. I think it more fun not to strain out the sloes but serve it from the bottle with them still in; it will keep with the sloes in for two or more years.

Sloe Jelly

2 kg (4 lb) sloes
6 dl (1 pint) water
2 kg (4 lb) sugar

Pick the sloes when fully ripe. Wash well and get rid of any bits of leaves. Put into a pressure cooker and cook with 6 dl (1 pint) of water for 5 minutes at high pressure or in open pan for about 40 minutes. Pour into a jelly bag and allow the liquid to drip through overnight. Warm the sugar and then add to the fruit juice. Boil until it reaches setting point, which takes about half an hour or so.

Recipe from Jenny Stone.

Sloe and Apple Cheese

1.2 kg (3 lb) apples
3 dl (½ pint) water
Sugar
900 g (2 lb) sloes

The apples may be a mixture of eaters and cookers, and windfalls are fine, if all the bruised parts are discarded. Wash the apples and sloes and drain them well. Cut up the apples without peeling or coring them. Put into a preserving pan with the water and simmer until the apples are soft and broken. Add the sloes and continue simmering until they are soft. Put through a sieve and weigh the purée. Allow 450 g (1 lb) sugar to each 450 g (1 lb) of purée. Stir in the sugar over a low heat until it has dissolved completely. Bring to the boil and then simmer, stirring well until the mixture is thick, which will take about 1 hour. Pour into sterilized jars with straight sides and cover. The flavour of sloes goes well with cold meat, particularly game.

Recipe from Mary Norwak.

Sloe Wine

1.2 kg (3 lb) sloes or bullace
1 kg (2.2 lb) sugar
2 oranges
4½ litres (1 gallon) water
Yeast
1 campden tablet

Boil the sloes in half of the water for 20 minutes, crushing them with a wooden spoon to break the skins, then strain off the solids and put the liquid in a plastic bucket. Start the yeast. Boil the sugar in the other half of the water until it has dissolved and squeeze in the juice of the two oranges, adding the crushed campden tablet. When it has all cooled down, add the yeast and leave to ferment in the bucket for four days before transferring to a fermentation jar. Leave it to ferment until it clears, about 3 months, then transfer to bottles. It improves a little on keeping and may have a better flavour a year later.

The taste of the wine will be enormously affected by the quality of the sloes; some years the results will be extremely dry and need sweetening with a little sugar syrup before drinking.

Making sloe gin. Old railway embankments are good places to gather sloes. Photographed October 20.

Cooking ceps with paprika. Photographed September 26.

Cooking haggis-stuffed ceps. Photographed August 24.

Ceps with Paprika

SERVES FOUR
450 g (1 lb) ceps
1 small onion, chopped
1 small clove garlic, chopped
50 g (2 oz) butter
1 large tomato, skinned, seeded and chopped
1 teaspoon mild paprika
Salt
4 tablespoons sour cream, room temperature
Lemon juice

If the ceps are large, cut them into convenient-sized pieces. Cook the onion and garlic gently in the butter until they are soft and golden. Stir in the tomato and bubble everything together for a moment or two before adding the paprika and then the mushrooms. Cover and cook for 3 minutes. Remove from the heat and add salt to taste. Put the pan back on the stove and stir in the sour cream. It should be allowed to boil gently and thicken with the sauce. Season with lemon juice to taste and serve immediately, preferably in the cooking vessel.

I got this fabulous recipe from Jane Grigson's book *Mushroom Feast*. Mrs Grigson got it originally from *Viennese Cookery* by Rose Philpott.

Stir-Fried Ceps

SERVES TWO-FOUR
250 g (8 oz) ceps
1 large onion, chopped
1 green pepper, chopped
1 red pepper, chopped
250 g (8 oz) tomatoes, quartered
Salt and pepper, olive oil
Soy sauce to taste

Wash and slice ceps, removing the pore layer if it has started to go green. Fry in olive oil for about 5 minutes. Add onions, peppers and tomatoes and fry for a further 10 minutes, stirring continuously. Add salt and pepper and soy sauce according to taste. Serve immediately. This makes a succulent stir-fry which is delicious served on its own or as a vegetable with grilled meat.

Stuffed and Baked Cep

Hors d'oeuvres
SERVES THREE
3 large ceps
4 slices of bacon, chopped
½ small pepper, red or green, chopped
Small clove of garlic
1 haggis sausage

Wash the ceps carefully, removing spongy part if green. Cut away any buggy bits and put the stalks to one side. Prepare the stuffing by frying the bacon with a dribble of oil or dripping if you've got it. Chop up a small piece of garlic very finely and half a small pepper, fry everything until brown and crisp, then add the meat of one haggis sausage (having carefully removed skin). Pile the mixture into the ceps and bake in a hot oven (220°C, 425°F, Mark 7) for about 15 minutes or until mushrooms feel soft when prodded.

This recipe is from Nicky Foy who adapted it from a recipe in Jane Grigson's *Mushroom Feast*. The original suggested using any good quality sausagemeat and Nicky had the idea of using haggis when staying in Scotland; ceps were plentiful and so was haggis!

Cep. Photographed August 20.

Summer boletus. Photographed July 29.

Charcoal Grilled Ceps

Remove the stems from good, firm caps of boletus, insert a clove of garlic or a shallot in place of the stem, add pepper, salt, a dash of oil and a quarter of lemon. Seal in aluminium foil and cook for about 15 minutes over a charcoal grill. An exciting accompaniment to any barbecue.

This recipe is adapted from *Mycologie du Goût* by Marcel V. Locquin.

Colin aux Ceps

SERVES TEN-TWELVE
2 kg (4 lb) fresh hake
450 g (1 lb) ceps
1 bottle Muscadet
1 carrot, sliced
1 stick of celery, sliced
1 onion, sliced
4 shallots, chopped
3 cloves of garlic, chopped
1 tablespoon vinegar
50 g (2 oz) cheese, grated
125 g (5 oz) butter, softened
4 egg yolks
Olive oil and a little butter
Bay leaf
Parsley, basil, thyme –1 teaspoon of each
Saffron, tarragon, fennel, chevril–1 teaspoon of each
5 teaspoon tomato purée

Cut the hake into cutlets. In a saucepan place the Muscadet, onion, carrot, celery, parsley (reserving a little parsley for later), basil, thyme, bay leaf, salt, pepper and a pinch of saffron. Bring to the boil and cook until vegetables are tender. Cool. Immerse cutlets. Poach them gently in a moderate oven 180°C (350°F, Mark 4) for

15-18 minutes. Remove and keep warm, Slice ceps and fry in a mixture of butter and oil with chopped shallots and garlic. Cook for 5 minutes and add the chopped parsley, the vinegar, 1 clove garlic, pinch of chopped tarragon and pinch of chopped fennel. When well reduced add mushroom liquid. Simmer for 10 minutes, then strain. You need 2 dl (1 gill) of liquid to add to bowl containing the egg yolks. Whisk until thick over boiling water. Add the softened butter, tomato purée, chopped tarragon, chervil and fennel. Arrange the fish in shallow dish, surrounded by ceps, sprinkle with grated cheese and brown under the grill. Cover with sauce and serve.

This recipe was given to me by Irene Palmer.

Cep *Boletus edulis* Bul. ex. Fr. Probably the most sought-after fungus in Europe for its fine flavour and texture, ceps can be found from midsummer to early winter, growing near trees and especially favouring warm wood edges, grassy clearings or ridges.

The word *Boletus*, by which the whole group is known, comes from the Greek word *bolus,* a lump. The cep has no gills like a field mushroom but under the cap is a mass of tubes which end in tiny pores giving it a spongy appearance. In a young, fresh specimen the pores will appear white but as they age they turn yellowish. If the pores are yellowish, they are best not eaten. They can easily be detached by peeling them away from the cap.

Summer Cep *Boletus aereus* Bull ex Fr. Usually found with either beech or oak trees in the late summer or early autumn. The cap is normally much darker than the ordinary cep but it is equally good to eat, if not better! Cook as ceps.

Bay Boletus *Boletus badius* Fr. Rather smaller then the cep, it can be found in conifer or mixed woods and is usually free of the grubs that bedevil the ordinary cep. Good to eat. Cook as ceps.

Bay boletus. Photographed October 2.

Slippery Jack. Photographed September 28.

Slippery Jack *Suillus luteus* (Fr.) S.F.Gray. I have adopted the American name for this fungus as we do not have a good English name for it. There are quite a few species in this group (Suillus) which are edible but this is the largest of them. They all grow in association with conifers of one sort or another; this one is generally with pines, as is *Suillus bovinus* (Fr.) O. Kuntze. The larch boletus *Suillus grevillei* (Klotsch) Sing. is always found with larches.

Slippery Jack and other members of the Suillus genus all have a sticky, glutinous coating on the cap which has to be removed by peeling. If cooked fresh they tend to be rather soggy and unpalatable but the flavour is very good, so the answer is to do as the middle Europeans do: peel and dry them and then, when you come to use them, powder the dried pieces and make a soup or add them to casseroles.

Dried Slippery Jack Soup

SERVES SIX
50 g (2 oz) butter
2 medium-sized onions, roughly chopped
1 large potato, diced
¼ litre (½ pint) dried Slippery Jack mushrooms
4 sticks of celery, sliced
1½ litres (2½ pints) stock (or water used to soak dried mushrooms)
Salt and pepper
Pinch of mixed herbs or thyme
Parsley to garnish

Melt the butter, add the chopped onions and sauté for 5 minutes. Add the potato, mushrooms and celery and continue cooking for a further 5 minutes. Add the stock and herbs to vegetables and simmer for 30 minutes. Liquidize and reheat. Serve garnished with parsley.

Orange birch boletus. Photographed September 28.

Orange Birch Boletus *Leccinum versipelle* (Fr. & Hok) Snell. It can be quite common in birch woods or in association with single birches and is much taller than the other species; the cap can grow to 20 cm (8 in) across. Discard most of the stem. This species turns blackish when cooked but is good to eat, especially in conjunction with the other types of cep.

137

Hazlenut nougat and meringues. Photographed October 10.

Hazel *Corylus avellana* L. The hazel is common throughout the British Isles, occurring in woods, scrub and hedges. It flowers from December to April and the nuts are borne from late August to October.

The English name is derived from the Anglo-Saxon 'haesel knut', from 'haesel', a hat or cap, and thus meaning a cap-nut or nut enclosed in a cap. The tree was cultivated by the Romans and the numerous references to it in early Gaelic literature and poetry suggest that it provided an important source of food in the Celtic diet.

In England, nutting was formerly a family occasion and until the First World War many village schools closed on Holy Cross Day (September 14) and the holiday was spent nutting. However, it was considered dangerous to go nutting on Sunday for one was likely to encounter the Devil on this day, although he usually appeared in friendly guise and held down branches of the tree for the nutters. A good crop of nuts seems to have been a bad portent – 'the more hazelnuts, the more bastard children', or in the Midlands, 'many nuts, many pits (graves)'.

The Celts associated the tree with fire and fertility and it was thought by many to ward off evil. A double hazelnut carried in the pocket would cure toothache, while a hazel twig cut on St John's Day or Good Friday was certain to make a successful divining rod. The leaves increase milk yield if eaten by cows. It is best to pick hazelnuts in late September as a compromise between the poor taste of early nuts and the loss to squirrels and jays later on.

Hazlenut Meringue

SERVES SIX
75 g (3 oz) hazlenuts
75 g (3 oz) ground almonds
6 egg whites
3 dl (½ pint) double cream
Icing sugar
350 g (12 oz) castor sugar
Fresh or frozen fruit

Chop the hazelnuts finely, preferably in a blender, and mix well with the almonds. Whisk the egg whites to stiff peaks. Add half the sugar and whisk again until the mixture is stiff and shiny. Fold in the remaining sugar and the nuts. Brush three, 25 cm (9 in) sandwich tins lightly with oil and line with circles of baking parchment. Brush the lining paper with oil. Put the mixture in the tins and spread lightly with a spatula to the edges of each tin. Bake at 170°C (325°F, Mark 3) for 45 minutes. Leave in the tins for 5 minutes and then turn on to cooling racks, carefully removing the paper from the bases. Leave until cold. Whip the cream stiffly. Assemble the layers of meringue with whipped cream and chosen fruit in between. Dust the top thickly with icing sugar.

A scrumptious recipe from Mary Norwak. I usually make up individual-sized meringues.

Hazlenut Nougat

Enough for about 20 nibbles
225 g (8 oz) hazlenuts
225 g (8 oz) sugar
225 g (8 oz) liquid glucose
100 g (4 oz) honey
1 egg white
3 tablespoons water

Place the water, sugar, glucose and honey in a pan and bring slowly to the boil, watching constantly at first as it can quickly boil over. Meanwhile, beat the egg white in a large bowl until stiff. Spread the hazelnuts on a marble surface or on rice paper. Continue boiling the sugar until it almost reaches small crack stage, 135°C (260°F). Remove the pan from the heat and gradually pour the hot mixture into the bowl with the whipped egg white, whisking all the time. After 2 or 3 minutes it will turn pure white and start to stiffen. Keep on whisking until the whisk will hardly move it, then spoon the mixture over the nuts. Leave for an hour to cool and set.

The timing of the sugar and egg whisking is rather tricky but the result always tastes delicious even if you do take it a bit too far. I

Haw wine, or at least the haws being collected. Photographed October 15.

could not find a satisfactory recipe for making this dish and it took seventeen attempts before I finally got it right. A good tip is to take the telephone off the hook when you start – the telephone ringing mucked up my first effort!

Haws, Hawthorn berries *Crataegus monogyna* Jacq. Haws were not thought highly of in ancient times as early proverbs indicate. For example, in 1280, 'Ne wisdam nis not worth an hawe', and in 1399, 'An harlots sonne not worth an hawe'. However, the fruit is not completely valueless, for 'when all fruit falls, welcome haws'. Another old saying, 'Many haws, many snaws', foretells of severe winter following a heavy crop of haws. The fruits were eaten by the Highlanders when thoroughly ripe and in India the tree is cultivated for its fruit. In Kamchatka the natives ate the fruit and made a kind of wine by fermenting them with water. An excellent liquor can be made from hawthorn berries in brandy. The fruit ripens at the end of September but can also be gathered as late as November.

Haw Wine

2 kg (4 lb) berries
1 lemon
2 oranges
1 kg (2.2 lb) sugar, brown or white
4½ litres (1 gallon) boiling water
Yeast

Put the berries in a large bowl and pour over the boiling water. Let this stand, covered, for a week and stir daily. Strain on to the thinly peeled rinds and juice of the fruit, add the sugar melted in a little water and stir. When the mixture has cooled, add the yeast, cover and leave for 24 hours. Transfer to fermentation jar and ferment to finish.

From Frank Duke and Honor, Cawsand, Cornwall.

This makes a very delicate pink wine that seems to benefit from keeping. It needs the addition of pectin to keep it clear.

Haw Jelly

1 kg (2.2 lb) hawthorn berries
Juice of 1 lemon
6 dl (1 pint) water
Sugar

Clean all the stalks from the berries and put them in a pan with the water and lemon juice. Bring to the boil and then simmer for 45 minutes, stirring from time to time. Strain the pulp through a jelly bag overnight. Discard the pulp and measure the juice – for every 6 dl (1 pint) add 450 g (1 lb) of sugar – and heat gently until it comes to the boil. Continue to boil rapidly until a really firm setting point is reached (try it on a saucer). Pour the jelly into small moulds such as an ice-cube maker and leave to set. The end result is a stiff, delicately flavoured jelly that can be cut with a knife and served with coffee after dinner.

Cortinarius purpurascens ready to cook. Photographed October 20.

Honey fungus in the Forest of Dean. Photographed October 21.

Orange peel fungus is usually found growing on woodland paths. Photographed November 5.

Honey Fungus *Armillaria mellea* (Vahl, ex Fr.) Kummer. Quite common and usually found rather late in the autumn growing on or around the base of deciduous or coniferous trees, often in great clumps. It can upset you if eaten raw and must be well cooked. I like it fried with onions, then with a little tomato added and the mixture used to fill an omelette.

Cortinarius purpurascens (Fr.) Fr. Usually found near oak trees but it can grow in both deciduous and conifer woods in the autumn. I say in my *Mushrooms* book 'edibility unknown', but since publication many people have told me that this is a good edible species and I have tried it and found it rather tasty; also, and more to the point, it has no bad after-effects. They are a wonderful purple colour, but unfortunately this is rather lost in cooking. I cooked them with garlic, shallots and a glass of white wine and served them on toast.

Fairy Ring Mushrooms *Marasmius oreades* (Bolt ex Fr.) Fr. This is one of our most common mushrooms. It is often found on lawns and in pastures, occurring from spring through to winter. It tends to grow in rings which make a darker area of grass known as the 'fairy ring' from which it gets its English name. Great care should be taken in learning the characteristics of this mushroom as there is a small white one *Clitocybe rivulosa* that is deadly poisonous and could be confused with it. However, when there is no doubt, fairy ring mushroom will prove to be a good edible species. They dry very well and so can be easily stored. Being small, they are often used in soups and stews, dried and powdered.

Galerina mutabilis (Schaeff. ex Fr.) Orton. It grows in dense clumps on stumps or at the base of deciduous trees and when in a nice, fresh condition, it is good to eat. It can be found from spring right through to early winter.

Orange Peel Fungus *Aleuria aurantica* (Fr.) Fuckel. This grows on bare soil on paths and roadsides in autumn and early winter. Although it has only a slight, delicate taste its addition to mushroom dishes is worthwhile due to its striking colour.

Fairy Peppers

225 g (8 oz) freshly minced rump steak
4 green peppers
1 onion
100 g (4 oz) fairy ring mushrooms
½ teaspoon mixed herbs
½ teaspoon paprika pepper
Vegetable oil for frying

Finely chop onion and fry in oil until golden brown. Add the minced meat, mix well with the onions, add the rest of the dry ingredients and fry until cooked. Wash and slice the fairy ring mushrooms, add to mince, mix in and fry gently for 2-3 minutes. Remove from heat and drain off excess fat. Wash peppers, remove tops, cut out stems, then remove seeds from body of peppers and wash out. Fill peppers with mince filling, replace tops, wrap in foil and place in shallow dish. Bake in a moderate oven 180°C (350°F, Mark 4) for 1 hour.

This recipe comes from S. L. Shute.

Fairy peppers being prepared with fresh fairy ring mushrooms. Photographed September 29.

Rosehip soup and rosehip syrup in the background. Photographed October 14.

Common dog rose. Photographed October 14.

Rosa rugosa *is another good source of rosehips, often planted in gardens but naturalized in several places, especially near the coast. Photographed September 30.*

Wild Rose *Rosa canina* L. A common shrub throughout the British Isles, it is found in woods, hedges and scrub. The wild rose flowers from June to July and bears fruit from late August to November. The fruits should not be picked until they have been softened by the first frost but they are of little use after the end of October. The seeds of the hip are covered with tiny hairs and care should be taken to use a very fine jelly bag when straining cooked hips.

The popular English name of this wild rose is 'dog rose' and it has been suggested that this is founded on an ancient tradition that the root would cure the bite of a mad dog. However, a more likely explanation is that the name was originally 'dag rose', dag meaning a dagger and alluding to the large thorns. In the language of flowers the dog rose symbolizes pleasure mixed with pain. A rose has been worn as a royal badge since the 13th century, while the Chinese use the petals as a vegetable. Cupid is said to have given Harpocrates, the god of silence, a rose, to bribe him not to betray the amours of Venus. For this reason the rose became the emblem of silence and was carved on the ceilings of banqueting rooms to remind the guests that what was spoken *sub vino* was not to be repeated *sub dive*. From this, 'under the rose' or *sub rosa* means, in strict confidence.

The hips of the wild rose were eaten in ancient times in Europe when other fruits were scarce. Gerard, 1633, comments: '[the hips] maketh the most pleasante meate, and banqueting dishes, and tartes, and such like'. The pulp of the fruit, separated from the seeds and mixed with wine and sugar, was used as a dessert. In Germany they were the main ingredient of a preserve and in Russia and Sweden they were fermented to make a wine and also made into a sweet soup. Rose hips are said to contain four times as much vitamin C as blackcurrant juice and twenty times as much as oranges. The leaves have been used to make tea.

Nyponsoppa (Rosehip Soup)

SERVES SIX
6 dl (1 pint) rosehips
100 g (4 oz) sugar
25 g (1 oz) almonds
2½ litres (4 pints) water
1 tablespoon potato flour or maize flour

Rinse the rosehips, put them in cold water and boil until soft – about 2 hours. While cooking, stir the soup strongly now and again. Strain, add the sugar and the potato flour, mixed with a little water, and bring to the boil again. Cut the almonds into strips and decorate.

This recipe came to me from Sweden (where it is a popular winter dish) via Marie Louise Avery, whose mother is Swedish.

Rosehip Syrup

For 3-4 bottles
1 kg (2 lb) rosehips
3 litres (4½ pints) water
450 g (1 lb) sugar

Remove stalks and mince (or chop) rosehips (don't leave rosehips lying once they are prepared or you will lose the valuable vitamin C content). Have ready a pan containing 2 litres (3 pints) boiling water and add rosehips. Bring back to boil, remove from the heat and leave to infuse for 15 minutes. Ladle rosehips and liquid into a scalded jelly bag and allow the bulk of the juice to drip through. Return the pulp (from the jelly bag) to the saucepan and add remaining litre (1½ pints) boiling water. Re-boil, infuse again for 10 minutes and strain as before. Pour the juice into a clean saucepan and simmer until it measures about 1 litre (1½ pints). Add the sugar and stir to dissolve, then boil for 5 minutes. Pour the syrup, while still hot, into warm, clean bottles within 25 cm (1 in) of the tops. Push in new corks (previously boiled for 15 minutes) not too tightly and tie with string. Place the bottles in the deepest saucepan you have, either on a false bottom or on corrugated paper or newspaper, and fill with cold water to the level of the syrup. Bring slowly to the boil. Simmer for 5 minutes to sterilize, then remove from the pan. Remove string and press the corks firmly in. Dry the bottles and when corks are dry dip into melted paraffin wax to keep them air tight.

This recipe was give to me by Katie Stewart. Home-made rosehip syrup made like this is vastly superior to the manufactured variety; it is not only nice on its own, but makes a superb sauce for ice-cream.

Rosehip Wine

1 kg (2.2 lb) rosehips
1 kg (2.2 lb) sugar
Juice of 1 lemon and 1 orange
4½ litres (1 gallon) water
Yeast

Mince the freshly gathered rosehips (make sure you pick them after the first frost). Place the minced rosehips into bucket and pour on boiling water. Stir with long-handled spoon or rolling pin. Do not use your hand because of the itchy hairs inside the hips. Allow the must to stand for three days. Stir daily. It will be quite stiff to stir. Strain it through a wine bag. Make up the sugar syrup, add to wine juice and place it into a fermentation jar. Make up the yeast and allow to work, then add to the wine. Make up amount of liquid to within 3 cm (1 in) of the top of the jar with boiled, cooled water; fit air-lock. Leave to work until clear, then syphon into clean container and keep for another three months. By then it should be ready to drink but it improves if allowed to keep for a few more months. If you prefer your wine a little sharper, add grape tannin to taste.

Scallops with mushroom sauce. Photographed September 8.

Field Mushrooms *Agaricus campestris* L. ex Fr. Found in pasture land in the summer or autumn, they were, at one time, very common and could be bought in shops side by side with cultivated species. However, they have declined in recent years, I imagine mainly because so much of our old pasture has been ploughed but possibly because the use of weed killers and fertilizers has also taken its toll. When I was a child on my grandparents' farm we seem to have been able to pick them in vast quantities every year, but then the sun always shone in summer and it always snowed at Christmas time. Do not peel mushrooms unless they are old but wipe the caps with a dampish cloth and cut off the stem base. Field mushrooms are very good raw in salads, cooked in soups or baked in pies but the most traditional way of making use of them is as a catchup.

Mushrooms in Milk

SERVES FOUR
1 kg (2.2 lb) mushrooms
1 litre (1½ pints) milk
2 onions
Small branch of thyme
Cornflour
Pepper and salt

Peel and cut up the onions and fry for 3 minutes in a little butter. Clean the mushrooms with a damp cloth, cutting away buggy stems, then add them to the onions. Add the milk and bring it slowly to the boil in a large pan, making sure that it does not boil over. Add the leaves from the thyme sprigs and a little pepper and salt. Leave to simmer gently for an hour or more, then thicken with a little cornflour paste prepared in water. Adjust the seasoning and serve with croutons cooked in butter and flavoured with a little thyme.

This is how my grandmother, Sarah, served them day after day in season and I still love them this way.

Scallops with Mushroom Sauce

SERVES FOUR
8 scallops
225 g (8 oz) mushrooms
1 egg yolk
Breadcrumbs
Butter
White wine
Cornflour
Garlic
Pepper and salt
Thyme

Roll the scallops in breadcrumbs and then lightly fry in vegetable oil for 4 minutes. Clean the mushrooms, chop them into small pieces and fry in butter for 4 minutes. Drain off the juices and put the mushrooms aside. Now, make a paste with cornflour and the juices, flavour it with pepper and salt and as it thickens, add a little wine to flavour, keeping it at a smooth consistency. Add the lightly beaten egg yolk and cook for 4 minutes. Return the mushrooms to the sauce and heat for a further 4 minutes. Place the cooked scallops on the scallop shells and surround them with sauce. Add ground black pepper and sprinkle on a little chopped thyme, then grill for about 4 minutes and serve bubbling hot.

Agaricus bisporus, *the grandfather of the shop mushroom.*
Photographed October 16.

Agaricus langei *discolours red but is good to eat. Photographed September 5.*

Wood mushroom discolours yellow. Photographed October 15.

Agaricus bisporus (Lange) Pilat. Found in waste places like rubbish heaps, manure and potting heaps and roadsides. It is thought that this species is the parent of the many cultivated varieties. It often appears quite early in the spring but can occur through to autumn. Just as fine to eat as the field mushroom, it can be cooked in the same way.

Agaricus langei (Moller) Moller. Found in coniferous or beech woods, from late summer to autumn, it is one of the species which goes red when cut, all of which are delicious to eat. Another reddening one which is good to eat is *Agaricus silvaticus* Schaeff. ex Secr. The prince *Agaricus augustus* Fr also has reddish tints but it bruises yellow rather than red. Again, excellent to eat, especially in croustade. It can be found in late summer or autumn in coniferous or deciduous woods and it smells strongly of burnt almonds.

Horse Mushroom *Agaricus arvensis* Schaeff. ex Secr. It can grow to an enormous size and is found in pastures where it grows in rings, some of which may be many metres across; it also grows at wood margins and in thickets. Horse mushrooms bruise and discolour yellow and have a smell of aniseed. It can be found from summer to autumn.

Wood Mushroom *Agaricus silvicola* (Vitt.) Peck. Another mushroom which yellows when bruised or with age, it can be found in coniferous or deciduous woods and smells of aniseed. To make sure of identification cut one or two fresh, young specimens and make sure that they do not show yellow in the flesh at the base of the stem. If it does show yellow at the stem base it may be the yellow stainer *Agaricus xanthodermus* Genevier which can cause extreme stomach upset in some people.

Mushroom Tart in Puff-paste

(My simplified version below)
'You must make a Cullis with the Slabs and Slices of Ham (a thick broth), then take a Quart of fresh buttons and toss them up in your Cullis of Mushrooms thick as Cream, then sheet a dish with Puff-paste and put in your mushrooms, and then strew some Crumbs of Bread over the top as thick as a half Crown, and sprinkle it, melted Butter and Yolks of Eggs, until you have covered your Crumbs and then bake it and cut a Piece out of the Top, and put in some of your Cullis, then shake it and serve away, squeeze in the Juice of an orange.'

This is an excellent recipe from Carter, 1736.

Mushroom Tart

(My version of Carter's ancient recipe)
SERVES FOUR
1 small bacon corner
450 g (1 lb) mushrooms
2 egg yolks
Pepper
Puff pastry
Breadcrumbs (home-made)
Cornflour

Cut the meat from the bacon bone and simmer the bone and the meat together for 1½ hours to make a stock. Clean the mushrooms, chop into medium-sized pieces and place in a saucepan. Add sufficient stock to just cover them and also pick out the nice pieces of the boiled ham and add to the mushrooms. Simmer without a lid (to reduce the liquid) for 30 minutes, then thicken with a little cornflour. Take the pan off the heat, add pepper and the egg yolks and stir carefully.

While this is going on make your puff pastry, roll out to a thickness of 3-4 mm (⅛ in) and line a round flat tin, 25 cm (10 in). Pour the mixture over the pastry, top with a good sprinkle of breadcrumbs and bake for 30 minutes at 200°C (400°F, Mark 6). Serve with a quartered orange so that the juice can be added to taste.

Horse mushrooms in a delicious croustade. Photographed September 5.

Horse Mushroom Croustade

SERVES-SIX
Croustade:
100 g (4 oz) soft breadcrumbs
100 g (4 oz) ground almonds or other nuts
50 g (2 oz) butter
100 g (4 oz) flaked almonds, pine kernels or hazelnuts
1 clove garlic, crushed
½ teaspoon mixed herbs

Topping:
450 g (1 lb) mushrooms
50 g (2 oz) butter
2 heaped teaspoons flour
4.5 dl (¾ pint) milk
Salt, pepper and nutmeg
4 tomatoes
1 teaspoon chopped parsley

Croustade: mix together breadcrumbs and ground nuts and rub in butter, cut into small pieces. Add flaked almonds, garlic and herbs. Mix together well and press down into an ovenproof dish, making a layer about 1½ cm (½ in) thick. Bake at 230°C (450°F, Mark 8) for 15-17 minutes until golden brown.
Topping: wash and slice mushrooms, sauté in butter until tender, add flour and when it froths remove from heat and stir in milk.

Return to heat, stir until thickened, then season. Spoon mixture on top of croustade, top with skinned and sliced tomatoes and a little salt, pepper and nutmeg. Return to oven for 10-15 minutes. Serve decorated with parsley.

Catchup of Mushrooms

'Take a Stew-pan full of the large flap Mushrooms, and the Tips of those you wipe for Pickling; set it on a slow Fire, with a handful of salt; they will make a great deal of Liquor, which you must strain, and put to it a quarter of a pound of Shallots, two Cloves of Garlick, some Pepper, Ginger, Cloves, Mace and a Bay-leaf; boil and scum it very well; when 'tis quite cold, bottle, and stop it very close.'
  Kettilby, 1728.

Mushroom Pickle

Button mushrooms only should be used to make this pickle. Stalk, wash and dry them thoroughly, then salt, to draw out moisture. Cook them slowly in the liquid which the salt has drawn out. Continue cooking until this liquid has evaporated, then season the mushrooms to taste with mace and pepper. Cover with vinegar and bring the whole to the boil. Boil slowly for a few minutes and let cool slightly before pouring into bottles or jars. When the pickle is cold, tie it down making the jar airtight.
  From *Complete Home Cookery* published by Fleetway House.

Chestnuts and delicious, fresh marrons glacés. Photographed October 27.

Sweet Chestnut *Castanea sativa* Mill. The generic name 'Castanea' is derived from the town Castanis in Thessaly where the tree grew in great abundance. The tree is indigenous in south-west Asia but was widely introduced in southern Europe by the Greeks, and in Britain by the Romans. The nuts are such a good source of food that in some Mediterranean countries they are a staple food, often dried and ground into flour. In the Apennine Mountains, in Savoy, Morea, Sicily, Madeira and the south of France, the poorer people used to subsist largely on a diet of chestnuts. Nor were they valued only by the poor. The Persian nobility, according to Xenophon, were fattened on chestnuts, while coffee houses in Lucca, Pescia and Pixtoga served delicious pâtés, muffins and tarts made of chestnuts.

They may be boiled, roasted, made into puddings, cakes, bread or porridge. In Europe, even the flowers are not neglected. John Evelyn tells us that: 'They also made Fritters of Chestnut-flower which they wet with Rosewater, and sprinkle with grated Parmegiano, and so fry them in fresh Butter, a delicate.'

However, roasting chestnuts in front of an open fire on a frosty winter evening takes a lot of beating. Remember to prick the skins first, unless you want to entertain the company with a minor war!

Chestnut Stuffing for Roast Turkey

900 g (2 lb) fresh chestnuts
1 minced turkey liver
700 g (1½ lb) pork sausage meat
75 g (3 oz) butter
1 onion
A glass of brandy
Pinch mixed spice
Salt and pepper

Split the chestnuts to avoid them exploding and heat for a few minutes in a hot oven, then peel, making sure to get rid of the bitter, inner peel. Cover the chestnuts with water and boil for 15 minutes or until tender. Strain and then mince into a large bowl, mix in the liver and sausage meat and flavour with spice and plenty of pepper and salt.

Heat the butter in a small pan, sauté the onion until soft but not brown, add to the large bowl, mix in the brandy and using your

hands fill the inside of the turkey.

I have adapted this recipe from Katie Stewart's *The Times Cookery Book*.

Marrons Glacés

Split fresh chestnuts and boil them in their skins for a few minutes to make it easy to skin them, remove the skins and boil for about 20 minutes to soften them. Drain off the water, cover with a sugar syrup and simmer slowly for one hour making sure they do not catch or boil over. Remove the chestnuts from the sugar solution and coat them thickly with sugar, then bake them in the oven for a few minutes. When you take them from the oven, squeeze a drop of lemon juice on each and dust them with castor sugar.

Chestnut Soup

SERVES FOUR (HUNGRY ONES)
450 g (1 lb) chestnuts
6 dl (1 pint) milk
1 teaspoon black pepper
½ teaspoon nutmeg
1 onion
1½ dl (¼ pint) stock
½ teaspoon mace
2 tablespoons oil

Boil the chestnuts in water to cover for half an hour and then remove the skins. Purée the chestnuts in a liquidizer, adding a little stock as needed. Cut up the onions rather finely and fry in oil, then add the stock, followed by the chestnut purée, and simmer until it starts to thicken. Stir often. Add half the milk and continue to simmer for 5 minutes, then add the rest, stirring frequently. Add spices, pepper and a little salt and cook for another half an hour or so. Serve as a main course soup with fresh bread.

From Jenny Stone.

Chestnut Flour (Farine de Châtaigne)

This is traditional in Corsica where chestnuts are plentiful and money is scarce; in the last war the whole population was practically sustained by it.

Collect the chestnuts as soon as they have fallen and store them in a

Beech mast. In a good year they can be found in vast quantities. Photographed October 5.

Acorns can be gathered with ease. Photographed October 20.

warm, dry room for about six weeks. In Corsica they have a little hut for this purpose called a *séchoir*. When they are thoroughly dried out, peel them and grind them into as fine a flour as you can. The flour will be yellow and rather sweet, and it is also rather 'heavy' so that it is normally used *moitié, moitié*, half and half, with ordinary flour to give it lightness and allow it to rise. Although grinding the chestnuts is a laborious job (unless you have a flour mill), it is well worth it in the end as the cakes and beignets made from the flour have a most interesting flavour. I used a grindstone pestle and mortar to do my grinding.

Beignets de la Farine de Châtaigne

225 g (8 oz) chestnut flour
225 g (8 oz) plain flour
Salt
Light cooking oil
Water

Mix the two flours and a good pinch of salt together and sieve into a bowl. Make a well in the middle and gradually mix in water until you have a rather wet, pancake-like mixture. Heat oil to a depth of 2 cm (1 in) in a frying pan until it starts to smoke, then spoon good-sized dollops of the dough into the pan and cook rapidly. Dust with a little sugar and serve red hot.

Corsican Flour Cake

225 g (8 oz) chestnut flour
225 g (8 oz) plain flour
6 eggs
2 small pots of plain yoghurt
5 teaspoons baking powder
2½ yoghurt pots of sugar
1 yoghurt pot of light oil (not olive)
Large pinch of salt
Zest of one lemon
100 g (4 oz) raisins
Rum

Put the raisins to soak in rum. Sieve and mix together the flours, add salt, sugar and baking powder and mix well. Break the eggs and stir into the flour with a wooden spoon, then add the yoghurt and oil. When all is nicely mixed to a smooth consistency strain the rum from the raisins and stir them and the lemon zest into the mixture. Transfer to a lightly greased cake tin and bake for 45 minutes in a medium to hot oven, 190°C (375°F, Mark 6).

All the information about chestnut flour and cooking with it came to me from Susan Alnutt who, with Dede, is a goat cheesemaker in Corsica.

Acorn Coffee

This is one the most traditional of the wild food recipes and yet it is not one that is much used. Acorns contain a large amount of tannin and when eaten raw they have a bitter taste and an astringent effect on the mouth. North American Indians of many tribes made use of acorns from one or other of the American oaks, but first they took steps to reduce the bitterness by soaking them in ashes and water or by burying them in the ground for some months.

I find that if you boil the acorns whole for 15 minutes you make it easier both to get the shell and peel off and reduce the bitterness. Boil and peel the acorns then split and dry them. After drying for a day or so, grind them in a coffee-grinder and roast them in the oven or under the grill, watching all the time to see they do not burn; they should be a good, brown coffee colour. Infuse about 1½ teaspoons per cup in boiling water for a few minutes before serving. The taste does not resemble coffee but it is quite pleasant with milk and sugar.

Beech *Fagus sylvatica* L. The beech is a native deciduous tree of south-east England, found especially on chalk, but elsewhere it is planted and often naturalized.

Beech bark was thought to be deadly to snakes while beech tea, made with lard, was a sure remedy for rheumatism. In Norway and Sweden the sawdust of beechwood used to be boiled in water, baked, and then mixed with flour to form bread.

Beech trees do not produce good mast (the encased nuts) every year but in favourable conditions an abundant mast may be produced every five to eight years. In times of famine the nuts have been eaten, and in France they have been roasted and served as a substitute for coffee. However, the nuts are very small and collecting and peeling sufficient for a meal is very arduous. The nuts, when well-ripened, yield 17-20% of a non-drying oil which has been used for cooking and as a fuel for oil lamps. It has also been used as a salad oil and to make butter and, two centuries ago, beechnut butter was made commercially from British beech mast. The mast should be gathered as soon as it falls, before it is taken by squirrels.

Summer truffles found in an oak wood. Photographed September 25.

Perigord truffles found near Algin in France. Photographed November 5.

White truffles found in the Piedmont area, Italy. Photographed November 8.

White helvellas. Photographed October 13.

eggs; salads – the nutty, mushroomy touch plus the strong aroma give real distinction; open sandwiches or smorgasbord of many kinds – in particular, those with pâté – are rendered spectacular with just the finest of fresh truffle slices.

Perigord or **Black Truffle** *Tuber melanosporum* Vitt. It can grow up to 15 cm (6 in) across but is not found in the British Isles and in the areas where it is found, mainly in France, it is much protected.

White Truffle *Tuber magnatium* Pico. Not found in the British Isles. It is the favourite of the Italians and is found in northern Italy. It can be as large as 15 cm across.

Red Truffle *Melanogaster variegatus* var *broomeianus*. 1-4 cm (½-1½ in) across, it is found on the surface or in the litter under beech trees, usually on chalk, at any time of year. Not a true truffle but related to the puff-balls, it was formerly sold in British markets as an alternative to the summer truffle.

Truffles on a Serviette

Truffles, bacon
White wine, chicken stock
Chopped parsley, thyme, bayleaf

Wash the truffles very carefully, using only fresh ones that are softish to the touch. Line a pan which has a good, tight lid with bacon slices, then place the truffles on top. Sprinkle with the herbs, barely cover with a half and half mixture of white wine and chicken stock, then lay a buttered paper over the top. Stew gently for 1 to 1½ hours, topping up the wine and stock as needed. Drain and serve hot in a folded serviette.

This classic recipe has been adapted from Mrs Beeton's *Book of Household Management*, 1861. Normally it would be made with Perigord or summer truffles but white or red truffles can be used.

Truffles en Croûte

Truffles (as many as you can find!)
Lean bacon slices, puff pastry

Halve or quarter large truffles to walnut size (use small ones whole), then wrap in a slice of lean bacon. Roll out the puff pastry

Summer Truffle *Tuber aestivum* Vitt. 2-8 cm (1-3 in) across, it should be looked for in chalk beech woods, usually just under the surface but sometimes half exposed, in late summer or autumn.

Mrs Beeton has this to say in her *Book of Household Management*, 1861. 'When the peasantry go to gather truffles, they take a pig with them to scent out the spot where they grow. When that is found, the pig turns up the surface with the snout, and the men then dig until they find the truffles. Good truffles are easily distinguished by their agreeable perfume; they should be light in proportion to their size, and elastic when pressed by the finger. To have them in perfection, they should be quite fresh as their aroma is considerably diminished by any conserving process.'

The fact is that the strong aroma of truffles contains the highest content of pheromone of any plant scent. Pheromone is the scent which animals give off as a sexual stimulant and the specific pheromone that truffles exude is practically the same as that given off by pigs in season and similar to that given off by dogs. It is for this reason that both pigs and dogs can be used to scent out truffles. Perhaps this also helps explain the high value that man places on truffles – could they have been a traditional aphrodisiac?

Raw, fresh truffles have a delicious, nutty flavour and a distinct, incredibly strong smell. If you keep a truffle with a bowl of eggs overnight, the eggs will begin to take on some of their flavour. Very fine slices cut with the slicing blade on a grater can be added to many prepared dishes: omelettes – truffles have a real affinity with

Hedgehog fungus served in flames. Photographed October 21.

and cut into 10 cm (4 in) squares. Place each bacon-wrapped truffle in the middle of a square of pastry, fold in the four corners one at a time to make a little parcel, seal the ends together and bake until golden brown.

Common White Helvella *Helvella crispa* Fr. Found on pathsides or roadsides in damp, deciduous woods in the autumn, it is quite common in some years. It can grow to as much as 25 cm (10 in) tall but is normally only about 10 cm (4 in) high.

White Helvella

Wash the helvellas carefully, discarding the bottom of the stem, dust with flour and fry in 25 g (1 oz) butter, with chopped garlic for 2-3 minutes. Add some mixed herbs, salt and pepper, plus ½ glass of dry white wine and cook until liquid is reduced by half – about 12 minutes.

André Marchand, the French author, in his *Champignons du Nord et du Midi*, 1973, says it is tasty cooked in the juice of roast beef. The result is pleasant and rather chewy.

Hedgehog Fungus *Hydnum repandum* L. ex Fr. Easily distinguished by having spines in place of gills, it can be found in either conifer or broad leaf woods from late summer until late autumn.

This is another species which is much sought after on the

Continent and is now sold in a few specialist shops in Britain. The flavour when raw is unpleasantly bitter and for this reason some people blanch them in boiling water before cooking, but if you have good, fresh specimens I think this is unnecessary.

Flaming Hedgehogs

750 g (1½ lb) hedgehog fungus
225 g (½ lb) shallots
Calvados
Cream
Oil and butter
Paprika
Salt and pepper

Clean and cut the hedgehog fungus into bite-sized pieces. It can all be eaten except the very bottom of the stem and it does not need peeling. Peel and finely chop the shallots, fry both in a mixture of oil and butter for 10-15 minutes, with a good flavouring of paprika, pepper and salt. Just before serving stir in a little cream and gently reheat. Serve in the hot pan (this means that it is best to use a rather heavy pan so that it holds the heat) and at the table pour over the dish a ladleful of preheated calvados which you light just before pouring.

This exotic recipe has been translated and adapted from *Mycologie du Goût* by Marcel V. Locquin, 1977.

Chicken and wood blewit pie is just one of the delicious ways of using these common mushrooms. Photographed November 15.

Wood Blewit *Lepista nuda* (Bull ex Fr.) Cooke. Common, and in some years prolific in beech woods, the season occurs at the end of autumn and early winter in woods, hedges and gardens. It has a strong perfumed smell which tends to persist in cooking. This mushroom should not be eaten raw.

Blue Legs or **Field Blewit** *Lepista saeva* (Fr.) Orton. Found in old pastures and meadows, usually growing in rings, in good years it is quite common. The season is late autumn up to Christmas. This is one of the few wild mushrooms, apart from the field mushroom, that has been eaten in Britain in the past and is known to have been sold in markets in Derbyshire.

Blewit and Chicken Pie

SERVES FOUR
450 g (1 lb) cooked chicken meat
350 g (12 oz) blewits of either kind
6 dl (1 pint) white sauce
Tarragon or mixed herbs
Pepper and salt
100 g (4 oz) short-crust pastry

Prepare a white sauce, seasoning well with herbs and salt and pepper. Slice the blewits and the chicken and layer them alternately in a deep pie dish. Roll out the pastry and cover, using an upturned egg cup in the centre to hold it up. Decorate imaginatively. Bake in a hot oven, 200°C (400°F, Mark 6) until the pastry is golden brown – about 45 minutes.

This recipe came to me from S. L. Shute and can be used for both wood and field blewits. If you don't have enough filling you can add a few slices of potato to make up the volume.

Sublime Blewits *(either species can be used)*
(Assemble in advance and toast just before serving.)

Sauté sliced, fresh blewits in butter over a very high flame and as they begin to brown add some finely chopped spring onions, then a little flour to thicken and some cream. It should all be reduced until nice and thick. Season well with salt and lots of coarsely ground black pepper and you can add a little sherry too but I prefer it without.

Remove the crusts from a thinly sliced, white sandwich loaf. Butter the bread and cover with mushroom paste. Roll up and fasten with a cocktail stick (lengthwise, rather like a kilt pin), place under grill and toast.

This is a variation of a Californian recipe in which ordinary button mushrooms were used. The rich flavour and meltingly light texture of the toast make this one of my very top recipes for a savoury.

From Irene Palmer.

Blue legs. Photographed November 4.

Yellow legs. Photographed October 8.

Horn of plenty, one of the best flavoured fungi. Photographed October 20.

Blewit Omelette

SERVES ONE
1 small onion
100 g (4 oz) blewits
3 tablespoons milk
1 tablespoon flour
Salt and pepper
2 eggs
Grated cheese

In butter, fry separately equal quantities of roughly chopped onion and blewit. Thicken with a little flour, which should be cooked for 1 minute, and milk to make a creamy, white sauce, season and then keep hot. Make an omelette with the eggs and when it is just setting pour in the blewit sauce, fold over and cover with grated cheese, then grill until the cheese is melting but not brown.

This 'winner' from Ray Cowell was first published in *The New Scientist.*

Horn of Plenty or **Black Trumpet** *Craterellus cornucopioides* (L. ex Fr.) Pers. It can be found in clusters amongst the leaf litter in deciduous woods, especially beech, in the autumn. Being black in colour they are very difficult to spot but once you find one you can usually gather quite a few by grovelling around on your hands and knees. It is well worth it if you do get a good collection as this inauspicious-looking little fungus has an unmatched flavour. It can be added to stews or soups as flavouring or to supplement and improve the flavour of any other mushroom dish you might be preparing. Horn of plenty, or black trumpet as it is also called, dries very easily and keeps well.

Black Trumpet Stir Fry

SERVES TWO-FOUR
225 g (8 oz) black trumpets
1 clove garlic, crushed
1 bunch spring onions
1 green pepper
225 g (8 oz) bean sprouts
Soy sauce to taste
Olive oil

Wash and roughly chop the black trumpets, dice the deseeded green pepper and thinly slice spring onions. Put olive oil in pan and heat. When the oil is hot add prepared ingredients, plus bean sprouts, crushed garlic, and soy sauce. Fry for 2-3 minutes, stirring continuously. Serve immediately.

Yellow Legs *Cantharellus infundibuliformis* (Scop) Fr. Found in all types of woods and copses in the autumn, it is quite common but easily overlooked. It is a good edible fungus which you may find growing in large numbers but if you only find a few they can be added to other collections for the pot. Easy to dry, it is only good to eat cooked as raw it is rather bitter.

Roots of wild carrot, parsnips and dandelion. Photographed December 16.

Dandelion roots should be dug in the winter. Choose year-old plants as the roots will have attained a decent size and should be slightly less bitter than younger specimens.

Dandelion Coffee

The name 'dandelion coffee' is a misnomer as the drink made from the roots is not and does not taste like coffee; however, it is quite a palatable drink that can be taken in place of coffee or tea.

Having collected a good supply of roots, clean them well and then dry them for about two days over a radiator or in an airing cupboard. Cut the dried roots into 1 cm (½ in) lengths and roast them; I do it in the pan under the grill. Make sure to turn them to get an even roast because just as with coffee you can make the flavour stronger by roasting them to a darker colour. Grind in an ordinary coffee grinder and make up in a jug using the sort of quantity you would use for instant coffee. Strain as you pour into cups. The flavour is nutty and rather bitter. I need a little sugar but then I have sugar in tea as well. They will keep in the unground, roasted state in a sealed jar.

Wild Parsnips *Pastinaca sativa* L. Wild parsnips are found scattered throughout England and are locally abundant, particularly on chalk and limestone in the south and east. They grow on roadsides and grassy waste places, are biennial and flower from July to September. The flowers are yellow and all parts of the plant have a strong, parsnip smell.

Parsnips have been cultivated as a root vegetable at least since Greek times, although they must have retained the characteristics of the wild species until the advantages of seed selection were understood. They gained enormous popularity with both Greeks and Romans; Emperor Tiberius had shipments of them regularly imported from Germany because their quality was considered superior to any other root vegetable, their food value being said to exceed that of all other vegetables except potatoes.

Wait until the first frost before digging up the roots as they will then be softer and sweeter. Ignore the large plants which have flowered during the summer; they are dead and finished. You need to dig the roots of the plants which are a year old and have not yet

Silverweed. The roots are at their best in autumn. Photographed June 10.

flowered. The taste of wild parsnip roots boiled or steamed is very good, but, to my mind, they would only be gathered if you were desperate, as they are very small.

Wild Carrot *Daucus carota* L. A biennial herb occurring throughout the British Isles but infrequent in the north, it grows in fields and grassy places, particularly on chalky soils and near the sea. It flowers from June to August. Collect roots from one-year-old plants at the end of the autumn.

The wild carrot has been put to many interesting uses: the reddish juice has been used as a food colouring; the syrup was made into a sweetening agent; carrot seed oil is used in perfumes; tincture of carrot seed is sometimes used in French liqueurs; and in times of shortages, roasted carrot roots have been substituted for coffee. In the Hebrides it was once a popular tradition for young girls to collect the roots before a dance and offer them to their fancied admirers as a delicacy.

It is a most tasty vegetable but it is extremely difficult to find enough sizable roots to make collecting worthwhile. Serve steamed or boiled with butter.

Oyster mushrooms, the fawn type. Photographed November 26.

Velvet shanks. Photographed on an elm stump. December 18.

Oyster mushrooms, the grey type. Photographed November 26.

Oyster Mushrooms with Fontina

SERVES FOUR-SIX
300 g (10 oz) oyster mushrooms
400 g (14 oz) fontina cheese
Knob of butter
½ clove garlic, crushed
Fresh parsley
Olive oil
A little milk or cream
Pepper and salt

Wash and slice the mushrooms. Chop the parsley. Melt the butter in a heavy pan, add the mushrooms, parsley, garlic and seasoning and sauté for 1-2 minutes, then remove from heat. Cover the bottom of greased ramekin dishes with olive oil. Place a first layer of the mushroom mixture in the dishes, cover with slices of fontina or some other, soft, melting cheese, then continue alternating mushrooms with fontina. Put into a pre-heated oven 130°C (250°F, Mark ½) and heat for approximately 40 minutes to allow the cheese to melt or until you have a bread-coloured crust on top. After 20 minutes cooking add some milk or cream to the dishes. This fondue of mushrooms with fontina, served very hot, makes an excellent first course.

Oyster Mushrooms à la Provençale

SERVES TWO-FOUR
300 g (10 oz) mushrooms
300 g (10 oz) tomatoes
1 glass white wine
1 onion
1 clove garlic
Olive oil
Parsley
Pepper and salt

Peel and finely chop the onion and put in an iron casserole on top of the stove with 2 tablespoons of good olive oil. Add a small, whole clove of garlic, the mushrooms cleaned and roughly chopped and fry furiously for 1-2 minutes. Now add the tomatoes, peeled, de-pipped and cut into pieces, the glass of white wine, pepper, salt and a generous quantity of chopped parsley; cover and simmer gently for 30 minutes. Remove the garlic clove and serve.

I have drawn this recipe from the book *Mycologie du Goût* by the French expert, Marcel V. Locquin, but I think it is the standard recipe from Escoffier. For those who like garlic, add 1 clove of crushed garlic a few minutes before serving.

Silverweed *Potentilla anserina* L. Silverweed is a perennial herb, common throughout the British Isles except in the Scottish Highlands. It occurs in waste places, roadsides, damp pastures and dunes and flowers from May until August.

The colour of the leaves of this plant gives it its common English name. Silverweed has been cultivated as a root crop from prehistoric times and the Anglo-Saxons used the roots boiled, raw or dried and ground into a meal for bread and porridge. Pechey, 1694, says, 'The Root of it, which they call Moors in Yorkshire, about Settle, are eaten by the Boys in Winter; for they taste sweet, and are as pleasant as Parsnips. Hogs dig them up, and eat them greedily.' In the Hebrides, in times of scarcity, the roots have supported the islanders for months. It is best to dig the roots in autumn, selecting a large, mature plant growing in soil which is not too heavily compacted. The roots should be dug carefully, washed thoroughly, and scraped to remove the dark outer skin.

I have had no joy eating this plant. The roots are generally too small to be worthwhile, so how whole populations of Scottish islanders lived on them I cannot imagine.

Oyster Mushroom *Pleurotus ostreatus* (Jacq. ex Fr.) Kummer. Can be found at any time of year but most common from the end of summer through to winter, it grows on stumps or old deciduous trees, especially beech. The colour varies from a beautiful blue-grey to fawn or flesh-brown.

Velvet Shank *Flammulina velutipes* (Curt. ex Fr.) Karst. Found growing in tiers on dead trees, especially elm, during December and January, it is a remarkable mushroom in that it can be completely frozen and then revive on thawing. Velvet shanks are rather small and normally used for flavouring stews and soups. Sautéed on their own they have a good flavour but a somewhat slippery texture.

155

Bibliography

Aarne, Antti. (1961) *The Types of Folktale,* Suomalainen Tiedeakatemia, Helsinki.

Addy, Sidney Oldall. (1895) *Household Tales with other Traditional Remains,* David Nutt, London.

Aihara, Cornellia. (1972) *The Chico-San Cookbook,* G.O.M.F., Oroville, California.

Allaby, Michael. (1975) *The Survival Handbook,* Macmillan, London.

Angeloglou, Maggie. (1977) *All About Herbs,* E. P. Publishing Ltd, W. Yorkshire.

Anonymous. (1873) *German National Cookery for English Kitchens,* Chapman & Hall, London.

Anonymous. (c. 1897) *Recipes for the Million: A Handy Book for the Household,* T. Fisher Unwin, London.

Austin, Thomas. (1888) *Two Fifteenth-Century Cookery-Books,* Early English Text Society, London.

Banks, Mrs M. Macleod. (1939, 1941) *British Calendar Customs: Scotland,* vols. II & III, Folklore Society, London.

Beech, F. W. (1954) *Wines, Syrups and Cordials,* National Federation of Women's Institutes, London.

Beedell, Suzanne. (1972) *Herbs for Health and Beauty,* Sphere Books, London.

Beeton, Isabella. (1861) *The Book of Household Management,* Ward Lock, London.
(1960) *Mrs Beeton's Cookery and Household Management,* Ward Lock, London.

Bickerdyke, John. (1886) *The Curiosities of Ale and Beer.*

Blakeborough, Rickard. (1911) *Wit, Character, Folklore and Customs of the North Riding of Yorkshire,* W. Rapp & Sons Ltd, Saltburn-by-the-Sea.

Boorde, Andrew. *See* Furnivall, F. J.

Brackett, Babette; Lash, Maryann. (1975) *The Wild Gourmet,* David R. Godine, Boston.

Bravery, H. E. (1961) *Successful Modern Winemaking,* Arco Publications, London.

Briggs, K. M. (1962) *Pale Hecate's Team,* Routledge & Kegan Paul, London
(1974) *The Folklore of the Cotswolds,* B. T. Batsford Ltd, London.

Brooke, Jocelyn. (1952) *The Flower in Season,* The Bodley Head, London.

Buchner, Greet. (1979) *Alternative Cooking,* Thorsons Publishers Ltd, Wellingborough.

Bullock, Helen. (1952) *The Williamsburg Art of Cookery or, Accomplish'd Gentlewoman's Companion: Being a Collection of upwards of Five Hundred of the most Ancient & Approv'd Recipes in Virginia Cookery* (publication of a much earlier, undated manuscript), Colonial Williamsburg Inc., Williamsburg, USA.

Bullock, Helen Duprey; McCully, Helen: Noderer, Eleanour. (1967) *The American Heritage Cookbook,* Penguin Books, Middlesex.

Campbell, Susan; Conran, Caroline. (1971) *Poor Cook,* Macmillan, London.

Carswell, Donald and Catherine (eds.). (1936) *The Scots Weekend and Caledonian Vade-mecum for Host, Guest and Wayfarer,* George Routledge & Sons Ltd, London.

Carter, Charles. (1730) *The Complete Practical Book: Or, A New System Of the Whole Art and Mystery of Cookery,* London.
(1736) *The Compleat City and Country Cook: or Accomplish'd Housewife,* London.
(1749) *The London and Country Cook: Or, Accomplished Housewife, containing Practical Directions and the best Receipts In all the Branches of Cookery and Housekeeping,* London.

Ceres. (1767) *The Lady's Companion: or, Accomplish'd Director In the Whole Art of Cookery,* John Mitchell, Dublin.

Christensen, Clyde M. (1943) *Common Edible Mushrooms,* University of Minnesota.

Clapham, A. R.; Tutin, T. G.; Warburg, E. F. (1962) *Flora of the British Isles,* Cambridge University Press, Cambridge.

Cleland, Elizabeth. (1759) *A New and Easy Method of Cookery,* Edinburgh.

Cobb, W. H. (1946) *Edible Fungi,* Arandar Books Ltd, London.

Coles, William. (1657) *Adam in Eden, or Nature's Paradise,* London.

Craig, Elizabeth. (1940) *Economical Cookery,* Collins, London.
(1953) *Court Favourites,* André Deutsch, London.
(1956) *The Scottish Cookery Book,* André Deutsch, London.
(1958) *Scandinavian Cooking,* André Deutsch, London.
(1965) *Cook Continentale,* Oliver & Boyd, Edinburgh.
(1969) *The Art of Irish Cooking,* Ward Lock, London.

Culpeper, Nicholas. (Undated modern edition) *Culpeper's Complete Herbal,* W. Foulsham & Co. Ltd, London.

Cumbria. (1965) *Recipes of Lakeland,* Dalesman Publishing Co. Ltd, Clapham via Lancaster.

Dalgairns, Mrs. (1849) *The Practice of Cookery adapted to The Business of Every-day Life,* Robert Cadell, Edinburgh.

David, Elizabeth. (1960) *A Book of Mediterranean Food,* John Lehmann Ltd, London.
(1951) *French Country Cooking,* John Lehmann Ltd, London.
(1960) *French Provincial Cooking,* Michael Joseph, London.
(1963) *Italian Food,* Penguin Handbooks, Middlesex.
(1970) *Spices, Salt and Aromatics in the English Kitchen,* Penguin Books, Middlesex.

Digbie, Sir Kenelme. (1669) *The Closet of the Eminently Learned Sir Kenelme Digbie Kt. Opened: Whereby is Discovered Several ways for making of Metheglin, Sider, Cherry-Wine, etc. Together with Excellent Directions for Cookerys: As also for Preserving, Conserving, Candying etc.,* London.

Dods, Margaret. (1827) *The Cook and Housewife's Manual,* London.

Duff, Gail. (1979) *Country Wisdom,* Pan Books, London.

Eley, Geoffrey. (1976) *Wild Fruits and Nuts,* E. P. Publishing Ltd, W. Yorkshire.
(1977) *101 Wild Plants for the Kitchen,* E. P. Publishing Ltd, W. Yorkshire.

Evelyn, John. (1679) *Sylva; or a Discourse of Forest Trees,* London.
(1699) *Acetaria, a Discourse of Sallets,* B. Tooke, London.

Farmers' Weekly. (1954) *Farmhouse Fare,* Hulton Press, London.

FitzGibbon, Theodora. (1980) *A Taste of the Lake District,* Pan Books, London.

Folklore Society. (1880/1881) *The Folklore Record,* vols. III & IV, Folklore Society, London.

Fowles, Gerry. (1980) *Straightforward Winemaking,* Gerry Fowles, Reading.

Furnivall, F. J. (ed.). (1870) *Andrew Boorde's Introduction and Dyetary, with Barnes in the Defence of the Berde,* Early English Text Society, London.

Genders, Roy. (1971) *The Scented Wild Flowers of Britain,* Collins, London.

Gennery-Taylor, Mr. (1957) *Easymade Wine and Country Drinks,* Elliot Right Way Books, Surrey.

Gerard, John. (1633) *The Herball; or General History of Plants very much enlarged and amended by Thomas Johnson,* London.

Grieve, Mrs M. (1931) *A Modern Herbal,* Jonathan Cape, London.

Grieve, Mrs M.; Oswald, E. (1925) *Fungi as Food and in Medicine.*

Grigson, Geoffrey. (1975) *The Englishman's Flora,* Paladin, Herts.

Grigson, Jane. (1975) *The Mushroom Feast,* Michael Joseph, London.
(1978) *Jane Grigson's Vegetable Book,* Michael Joseph, London.

Hargreaves, Barbara (ed.). (1971) *The Country Book,* Countrywise Books, London.
(1974) *The Second Country Book,* Hamlyn Publishing Group Ltd, London.

Harris, Ben Charles. (1973) *Eat the Weeds,* Keats Publishing Inc.,

Connecticut.

Hartley, Dorothy. (1969) *How To Enjoy Your Weeds*, Frederick Muller, London.

Heath, Ambrose. (1953) *Home-made Wines and Liqueurs*, Herbert Jenkins, London.

Hedrick, U. P. (1919) *Sturtevant's Notes on Edible Plants*, J. B. Lyon & Co., Albany.

Henderson, William. (1879) *Notes on the Folklore of the Northern Countries of England and the Borders*, Satchell, Peyton & Co. for the Folklore Society, London.

Hill, John. (1755) *The Useful Family Herbal*, London.
(1756) *The British Herbal*, London.

Hilton, Henrietta. (1964) *The Best of German Cooking*, Arlington Books, London.

Howe, Robin. (1953) *German Cooking*, André Deutsch, London.

Hyde, Molly. (1976) *Hedgerow Plants*, Shire Publications Ltd, Buckinghamshire.

Johnson, C. Pierpoint. (1862) *The Useful Plants of Great Britain*, William Kent & Co., London.

Jones-Baker, Doris. (1977) *The Folklore of Hertfordshire*, B. T. Batsford Ltd, London.

Jordan, Michael. (1976) *A Guide to Wild Plants*, Millington Books Ltd, London.

Kerr, Jessica. (1969) *Shakespeare's Flowers*, Longman, London.

Kettilby, Mary. (1728) *A Collection of above Three Hundred Receipts in Cookery, Physick and Surgery; For the Use of all Good Wives, Tender Mothers, and Careful Nurses*, London.

Laird, A. Bonnet. (1927) *The Old Master Cookery Book*, Herbert Jenkins Ltd, London.

Latham, Charlotte. (1878) *Some West Sussex Superstitions Lingering in 1878*, The Folklore Record 1:1-67, Folklore Society, London.

Leverett, Brian. (1979) *Winemaking Month by Month*, Prism Press, Dorset.

Locquin, Marcel V. (1977) *Mycologie du goût*, J. F. Guyot, Paris.

Loewenfeld, Claire; Back, Philippa. (1980) *Britain's Wild Larder*, David & Charles, Newton Abbot.
(1965) *Herbs for Health and Cookery*, Pan Books, London.

Losch Dr. (1907) *Les Plantes Médicinales*, Paris.

Mabey, Richard. (1972) *Food for Free*, Collins, London.

Madlener, Judith Cooper, (1977) *The Seavegetable Book*, Clarkson N. Potter Inc., New York.

Markham, Gervase. (1623) *Countrey Contentment or The English Huswife*, London.
(1623) *The English Huswife*, London.

Mauduit, Vicomte de. (1934) *The Vicomte in the Kitchen*, Stanley Nott, London.
(1939) *The Kitchen Companion*, Country Life Ltd, London.
(1940) *They Can't Ration These*, Michael Joseph, London.

McIlvaine, Charles; Macadam, Robert K. (1912) *One Thousand American Fungi*, The Bobbs-Merrill Company, Indianapolis.

Mead, William Edward. (1931) *The English Medieval Feast*, George Allen & Unwin, London.

Michael, Pamela. (1980) *All Good Things Around Us*, Ernest Benn Ltd, London.

Mitchell, Jan. (1955) *Lüchow's German Cookbook*, Hammond, Hammond & Co., London.

Mori, Kisaku. (1974) *Mushrooms as Health Foods*, Japan Publications Inc., Tokyo.

National Federation of Women's Institutes. (1968) *Unusual Preserves*, N.F.W.I., London.

O'Ceirin, Cyril and Kit. (1980) *Wild and Free*, Skilton & Shaw, London.

Ohsawa, Lima. (1974) *The Art of Just Cooking*, Autumn Press, Massachusetts.

Oswald, Ella. (1906) *German Cookery for the English Kitchen*, A. Siegle, London.

Paton, C. I. (1939) *Manx Calendar Customs*, William Glaisher Ltd for the Folklore Society, London.

Pechy, John. (1694) *The Compleat Herbal of Physical Plants*, London.

Perring, F. H.; Walters, S. M. (1976) *Atlas of the British Flora*, E. P. Publishing Ltd for the Botanical Society of the British Isles, Wakefield.

Peterson, Vicki. (1978) *The Natural Food Catalogue*, Macdonald & Jane's, London.

Plat, Sir Hugh. (1659) *The Garden of Eden*, London.

Ranson, Florence. (1949) *British Herbs*, Pelican Books, Middlesex.

Read, Miss. (1969) *Country Cooking*, Cookery Book Club, London.

Reekie, Jennie. (1976) *Traditional French Cooking*, Pan Books, London.

Rhoades, Sharon Ann. (1978) *Cooking with Sea Vegetables*, Autumn Press Inc.

Rhodes, Dennis. (1968) *In an Eighteenth Century Kitchen: A Receipt Book of Cookery, 1698*, Cecil and Amelia Woolf, London.

Richardson, Rosamund. (1980) *Hedgerow Cookery*, Penguin Books, Middlesex.

Robinson, Matthew. (n.d.) *The New Family Herbal and Botanic Physician*, William Nicholson & Sons, London.

Roden, Claudia. (1968) *A Book of Middle Eastern Food*, Thomas Nelson, Surrey.

Rohde, Eleanour Sinclair. (1935) *Shakespeare's Wild Flowers: Fairy Lore, Gardens, Herbs, Gatherers of Simples and Bee Lore*, The Medici Society, London.

Roman, Liz. (1977) *A Fenland Village Cookery Book*, Wicken Fête Committee and the Wicken Society, Wicken, Cambridge.

Rosen, Ruth Chier. (1959) *Wurst you were here*, Richards Rosen Associates Inc., New York.

Schofield, Bernard. (1978) *The Urban Dweller's Country Almanac*, Cassell, London.

Scott, Amoret. (1979) *Hedgerow Harvest*, Oxford Illustrated Press, Oxford.

Seddon, George; Radecka, Helena. (1975) *Your Kitchen Garden*, Mitchell Beazley, London.

Simmonds, N. W. (ed.). (1976) *Evolution of Crop Plants*, Longman, London.

Simpson, Jacqueline. (1973) *The Folklore of Sussex*, B. T. Batsford Ltd, London.

Singer, Rolf. (1961) *Mushrooms and Truffles*, Leonard Hell, London.

Stewart, Katie. (1974) *The Times Cookery Book*, Pan Books, London.

Stobart, Tom. (1970) *Herbs, Spices and Flavourings*, David & Charles, London.

Sturtevant. *See* Hedrick, U. P.

Swann, Claire. (1980) *Nettles: Healers of the Wild*, Thorsons Publishers Ltd, Northamptonshire.

Turner, B. C. A. (1980) *Country Wines & Cordials*, Marshall Cavendish Editions, London.

Weiner, Michael. A. (1980) *Earth Medicine – Earth Food*, Collier Books, New York.

White, Florence, (1934) *Flowers as Food*, Jonathan Cape, London.
(1952) *Good English Food, Local and Regional*, Jonathan Cape, London.

Whitfield, Nella. (1960) *Cooking the German Way*, Spring Books, London.

Wise, Dorothy. (1973) *Home-made Country Wines*, Hamlyn Paperbacks, Middlesex.

INDEX